Microsoft BizTalk ESB Toolkit 2.1

Discover innovative ways to solve your mission-critical integration problems with the ESB Toolkit

Andrés Del Río Benito

Howard S. Edidin

BIRMINGHAM - MUMBAI

Microsoft BizTalk ESB Toolkit 2.1

First published: July 2013

Production Reference: 1190713

Published by Packt Publishing Ltd.
Livery Place
35 Livery Street
Birmingham B3 2PB, UK.

ISBN 978-1-84968-864-2

www.packtpub.com

Cover Image by Prashant Timappa Shetty (sparkling.spectrum.123@gmail.com)

Credits

Authors

Andrés Del Río Benito

Howard S. Edidin

Reviewers

René Brauwers

Abdul Rafay

Jean-Paul Smit

Acquisition Editor

Grant Mizen

Commissioning Editor

Poonam Jain

Technical Editors

Vrinda Nitesh Bhosale

Dominic Pereira

Amit Ramadas

Project Coordinator

Deenar Satam

Proofreader

Mario Cecere

Indexers

Hemangini Bari

Mariammal Chettiyar

Tejal R. Soni

Graphics

Valentina D'silva

Production Coordinator

Melwyn D'sa

Cover Work

Melwyn D'sa

About the Authors

Andrés Del Río Benito has been working with BizTalk since 2004, and all the way through all its versions until BizTalk 2010. Over the years, he has played the role of developer, consultant, architect, and development lead in different projects, and has also been the official BizTalk trainer for different teams across Accenture CIO and Avanade Spain.

Apart from working with BizTalk, he has spent many years in the Avanade and Accenture CIO Enterprise Architecture teams involved in different initiatives not only around BizTalk but also many other technologies along the Microsoft Stack. This was until he left Spain (and so Avanade/Accenture) with his wife to find new challenges in London; here, after spending some time as a BizTalk contractor for Microsoft UK, he currently works for BBC Worldwide as a Solutions Architect.

Howard S. Edidin is an independent BizTalk architect/consultant specializing in providing guidance and training for companies implementing BizTalk. He was first exposed to BizTalk about the time when "Soap on a Rope" was introduced by Microsoft. He didn't get a chance to use it, until BizTalk 2002 came along.

Most of Howard's BizTalk career has been in contract work, which has allowed him to utilize almost all of BizTalk's capabilities. Last year Howard established his own consulting company, the Edidin Group Inc. in order to expand the services he provides.

Howard has been very active in the BizTalk community. He has contributed several articles to the TechNet Wiki, provided answers to questions on the LinkedIn BizTalk Groups, contributes to several BizTalk Administration blogs, and maintains his own blog.

In addition to co-authoring this book, Howard was a co-author of *Microsoft BizTalk 2010 Administration Essentials* along with *Steef-Jan Wiggers, Andrés Del Río Benito*, and *Tord Glad Nordahl, Packt Publishing* and a technical reviewer for Packt Publishing on SOA Made Simple by Lonneke Dikmans and Ronald van Luttikhuizen.

Howard is married and resides in Libertyville, IL.

He was certified as an MCP in 1998, and is currently certified MCTS in BizTalk 2010.

I would like to thank my wife, Sharon, for allowing me the time to write this book. I especially would like to thank my good friend and co-author, Andres Del Rio, for his encouragement and collaboration.

About the Reviewers

René Brauwers started his IT career as a web developer/designer and was primarily engaged with building websites using classic ASP. Soon, his focus got more drawn towards developing client/server applications using the 3GL language Centura/Gupta Team Developer. Around the end of 2002, he got in touch with the EAI/B2B/B2C/BPM world, starting off with WebMethods and did this for the next three years with an occasional side step to .NET development. This occasional side step got him in touch with BizTalk Server in 2005.

Currently, he is employed as a senior Microsoft Integration consultant for Motion10 (http://www.motion10.com) in the Netherlands focusing on BizTalk Server and Windows Azure. René can be contacted via e-mail (rene@brauwers.nl), Twitter (@ReneBrauwers), LinkedIn (http://nl.linkedin.com/in/brauwers), or through his blog 'Me, Azure, .NET and BizTalk' (http://blog.brauwers.nl).

Special thanks go out to everyone actively participating in the Microsoft Integration space, my colleagues at Motion10, family, and of course my soon to be wife Miranda; words simply can't express my love for you.

Abdul Rafay has been working on integration with BizTalk and other Microsoft technologies for more than six years. He works as an Integrator in a Bank in Qatar where he is involved in architecture, design, development, and testing of integration solutions built on Microsoft platforms, which mainly includes BizTalk, WCF, and Windows Server AppFabric. You can visit his blog: `http://abdulrafaysbiztalk.wordpress.com`.

Abdul has a vast experience of integration projects in the banking domain, and has been involved in projects integrating banking applications with core banking systems and B2B partners. He has previously worked with the largest implementations of BizTalk in regions like United Bank Ltd. Pakistan, and SADAD in KSA.

Abdul is a three times Microsoft Most Valuable Professional (MVP) in BizTalk and likes to share his knowledge and technical expertise on his blog, MSDN, and other forums.

Other than Integration projects and BizTalk, Abdul has previously worked as a web developer on technologies such as ASP, ASP.NET, SharePoint, and open source web applications.

I would like to thank my fantastic wife, Hira, for making this project and my life successful. Thanks for your understanding, patience, and support which lead me to success. I would like to thank the Almighty God for giving me all what I have. I would like to thank all my friends who were there when I needed them and specially my in-laws. Thanks to all those who have contributed to my success and were part of my life.

Jean-Paul Smit grew up in a small town in the Netherlands, working in his parent's greenhouse. However, information technology caught him early and after graduation, he started to work in the greenhouse automation business in 1996. A few years later, he was involved in the first real Internet project at the Aalsmeer flower auction. From there Internet was the way to go and he switched jobs to work for the Dutch company Macaw, to work with Microsoft only technology. In 2004 he was introduced to Microsoft BizTalk Server, and from that moment he spent most of his time on application integration using this platform. After a couple of interesting projects he decided it was time for the next step, go freelance. Since 2008, he is working under his company name Didago IT Consultancy to help customers solve application integration challenges, not only using BizTalk server but also other technologies on the Microsoft integration stack such as WCF and SSIS. Among his customers are companies like Asics, KPN, and AkzoNobel.

He is the co-founder of the BizTalk Software Factory community project on Codeplex. This software factory assists with generating consistent BizTalk application structures in Visual Studio and supplying guidance while developing applications. The next step for BizTalk will be the move towards cloud computing and that inspired him to write some articles about BizTalk and Windows Azure.

www.PacktPub.com

Support files, eBooks, discount offers and more

You might want to visit www.PacktPub.com for support files and downloads related to your book.

Did you know that Packt offers eBook versions of every book published, with PDF and ePub files available? You can upgrade to the eBook version at www.PacktPub.com and as a print book customer, you are entitled to a discount on the eBook copy. Get in touch with us at service@packtpub.com for more details.

At www.PacktPub.com, you can also read a collection of free technical articles, sign up for a range of free newsletters and receive exclusive discounts and offers on Packt books and eBooks.

http://PacktLib.PacktPub.com

Do you need instant solutions to your IT questions? PacktLib is Packt's online digital book library. Here, you can access, read and search across Packt's entire library of books.

Why Subscribe?

- Fully searchable across every book published by Packt
- Copy and paste, print and bookmark content
- On demand and accessible via web browser

Free Access for Packt account holders

If you have an account with Packt at www.PacktPub.com, you can use this to access PacktLib today and view nine entirely free books. Simply use your login credentials for immediate access.

Instant Updates on New Packt Books

Get notified! Find out when new books are published by following @PacktEnterprise on Twitter, or the *Packt Enterprise* Facebook page.

Table of Contents

Preface

This book is meant to be a guide to the Microsoft ESB Toolkit 2.1. In this book, we will provide a high-level view along with detailed descriptions of the services and components that make up the Toolkit. Scenarios are provided to help you understand how these services and components can be used.

What this book covers

Chapter 1, ESB Toolkit, Architecture, and Features, provides us with an overview of the Enterprise Service Bus (ESB) and the architectural principles that define it.

Chapter 2, Itinerary Services, explains the conceptual definition of different services and processes that a message should go through to complete a business process.

Chapter 3, ESB Exception Handling, explores the ESB Exception framework, its components and services, and the benefits it provides.

Chapter 4, ESB Toolkit Web Services, explores the different services that the ESB provides and views a few scenarios.

Chapter 5, ESB Management Portal, shows us how to publish EndPoints into UDDI 3.0, and the use of the different parameterizations that we can do.

Chapter 6, ESB Toolkit Version 2.2 for BizTalk 2013, shows us what's new in the Toolkit, and explains how to install and configure it.

What you need for this book

You need the following to work with the examples given in the book:

- Microsoft BizTalk Server 2010 Developer or Enterprise Version
- Microsoft ESB Toolkit 2.1
- UDDI 3.0

Who this book is for

This book is primarily for experienced BizTalk Developers and Architects. IT Managers and Business Analysts would also benefit from this book.

Conventions

In this book, you will find a number of styles of text that distinguish between different kinds of information. Here are some examples of these styles, and an explanation of their meaning.

Code words in text, database table names, folder names, filenames, file extensions, pathnames, dummy URLs, user input, and Twitter handles are shown as follows: "These are instantiated using the `Microsoft.Practices.ESB.ExceptionHandling. ExceptionMgmt.CreateFaultMessage` method of the API within an exception handling block in an orchestration. This generates a new BizTalk message whose schema is `Microsoft.Practices.ESB.ExceptionHandling.Schemas.Faults. FaultMessage`."

A block of code is set as follows:

```
<?mso-infoPathSolution solutionVersion="1.0.0.346"
productVersion="11.0.6565"
PIVersion="1.0.0.0"
href=file:///\\localhost\publish\Microsoft.Practices.ESB.
ExceptionHandling.InfoPath.Reporting.xsn
name="urn:schemas-microsoft-com:office:infopath:
Microsoft-Practices-ESB-ExceptionHandling-InfoPath-Reporting:
http---schemas-microsoft-biztalk-practices-esb-com-exceptionhandling"
language="en-us" ?><?mso-application progid="InfoPath.Document"?>
```

New terms and **important words** are shown in bold. Words that you see on the screen, in menus or dialog boxes for example, appear in the text like this: "All the reports are accessible through the **Reports** link on the portal navigation bar, and can be filtered by application and by time range."

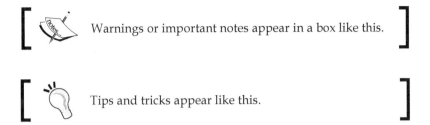

[Warnings or important notes appear in a box like this.]

[Tips and tricks appear like this.]

Reader feedback

Feedback from our readers is always welcome. Let us know what you think about this book—what you liked or may have disliked. Reader feedback is important for us to develop titles that you really get the most out of.

To send us general feedback, simply send an e-mail to `feedback@packtpub.com`, and mention the book title via the subject of your message.

If there is a topic that you have expertise in and you are interested in either writing or contributing to a book, see our author guide on `www.packtpub.com/authors`.

Customer support

Now that you are the proud owner of a Packt book, we have a number of things to help you to get the most from your purchase.

Errata

Although we have taken every care to ensure the accuracy of our content, mistakes do happen. If you find a mistake in one of our books—maybe a mistake in the text or the code—we would be grateful if you would report this to us. By doing so, you can save other readers from frustration and help us improve subsequent versions of this book. If you find any errata, please report them by visiting `http://www.packtpub.com/submit-errata`, selecting your book, clicking on the **errata submission form** link, and entering the details of your errata. Once your errata are verified, your submission will be accepted and the errata will be uploaded on our website, or added to any list of existing errata, under the Errata section of that title. Any existing errata can be viewed by selecting your title from `http://www.packtpub.com/support`.

Piracy

Piracy of copyright material on the Internet is an ongoing problem across all media. At Packt, we take the protection of our copyright and licenses very seriously. If you come across any illegal copies of our works, in any form, on the Internet, please provide us with the location address or website name immediately so that we can pursue a remedy.

Please contact us at copyright@packtpub.com with a link to the suspected pirated material.

We appreciate your help in protecting our authors, and our ability to bring you valuable content.

Questions

You can contact us at questions@packtpub.com if you are having a problem with any aspect of the book, and we will do our best to address it.

1
ESB Toolkit, Architecture, and Features

BizTalk Server has been around for quite a long time, evolving over the years and becoming one of the most complete and powerful middleware products in the market, helping thousands of companies to fulfill their requirements in terms of Systems Integration.

With such a powerful product and the flexibility it provides to implement integration solutions, it's more than useful to have at hand a set of architectural patterns and re-usable components. These will support our design and help us to reach the most successful result possible. And here's where the ESB Toolkit comes into the picture.

In this chapter, we will have an overview of:

- What is Enterprise Service Bus (ESB)
- What are the architectural principles that define an ESB
- How the ESB Toolkit helps to build better integration solutions
- What are the ESB Toolkit features and components

The content within this book is not meant to be a long dissertation about the different architectural terms and acronyms coined over time that lead into the definition of what an ESB is about. We will save you some time by going straight to the point of defining the basics of ESB so you can spend that extra time on enjoying a good BBQ.

Understanding the basics

An **Enterprise Service Bus** (**ESB**) is an architectural model that defines the patterns to integrate IT systems by interconnecting an ecosystem of loosely coupled and interoperable business services and components in an elastic way. The ultimate goal is to provide a flexible implementation of the enterprise business processes in such a flexible way that those processes can be efficiently adapted to the ever-changing circumstances of the enterprise.

In the following figure, we can see different example business processes that could be run within our ESB, as a set of decoupled business services or stages:

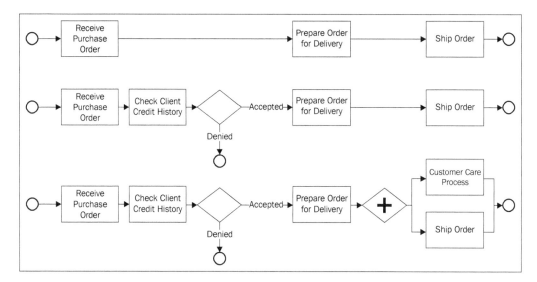

The VETRO pattern

In most cases, a business process is all about how information travels through the process and how it is handled along the way, and thus the ESB model predicates the integration of such business processes in terms of the five basic steps that conform to the **VETRO** pattern:

- **Validate**: This is usually the very first step of the information processing, where we ensure that the information received is in the format expected, although there can be other validation steps along the process. This validation against the mutually agreed service/data contracts ensures that the information flowing through the ESB is legitimate and compliant with the expectations of any system connected to the bus.

- **Enrich**: During this step, the information is enriched so it contains all the data required to continue its journey and provide a meaningful input to the target system.

- **Transform**: The information is transformed to the format the target system expects and understands. This step could happen as the information arrives at the ESB (where in this case the target system is the ESB itself) where the information would be transformed into a canonical format (quite often defined by the company's Enterprise Data Model), as well as when the information leaves the ESB, transforming it from the canonical format to the format expected by the target system.

- **Route**: In systems integration, the information intrinsically has to travel from one place to the other, and that is what happens during this stage. The next step the information needs to take is identified and the route is applied so the process can continue as expected.

- **Operate**: The business processes are all about triggering actions within the enterprise that achieve the mission the process is designed for. In this stage, the target system is delivered the input information so any required actions are taken and any expected outcomes are produced. In essence, the Operate step is the invocation of a target service or even an interaction with the target service.

The ESB receives messages from the systems connected to it and performs one or more of the steps mentioned previously. All those steps that define how a message needs to be handled by the ESB are defined as itineraries, that are a set of decoupled processing steps that doesn't necessarily know about the whole process the message just went through or is going to go through afterwards, but they just know what they have to do with the message they just received for processing.

This doesn't sound like rocket science or anything very new, but what the ESB adds to the pattern is the means to make all these stages along the process as **decoupled** and **configurable** as possible, so once a process is in place any further changes can be made with the smaller effort and the smallest impact possible on existing systems.

ESB capabilities

An ESB has different features and capabilities that support one or many of the elements of the VETRO pattern.

The main capabilities that support this model in the ESB are listed in the following table:

Capability	Mapping to VETRO	Description
Message Routing	---RO	Dynamic and configurable message routing allows flexible processes to be changed even at runtime
Connectivity	---RO	Adapters and other protocol transformation components facilitate the connections between heterogeneous systems
Exchange Patterns	---RO	Business processes usually require different message exchange patterns, such as synchronous/asynchronous, pub-sub, and so on
Transformation	--T-O	Systems that understand different data formats and structures require a man in the middle to help them talk to each other
Service Directory	--TRO	Loosely coupled service architectures require a centralized directory where consumers can find the service they need to use
Rules Dynamic Resolution	VETRO	The configurable and elastic behavior ESB predicates require a rule system that provides flexibility to the other capabilities of the system
Validation	V-T--	Information needs to be validated to ensure it complies with the definition of the business processes
Aggregation	-ET-O	The business processes are usually composed of multiple subprocesses that will be invoked to enrich and transform the information as the overall process runs
Service Orchestration	---RO	
Assured Delivery	---RO	Some features such as message queuing or assured delivery are required to ensure reliable and predictable execution of business processes

Capability	Mapping to VETRO	Description
Management and Governance	-----	We need to be able to configure and monitor the behavior of the processes so we are always on top of what is happening in our business
Security	-----	The execution of our business processes needs to rely on a security system that ensures that all the parties involved are who they claim to be and are allowed to take the actions they want to perform

If you have been working with BizTalk Server for some time or have some basic knowledge about its architecture and features, you will find that most of those cover these capabilities any ESB system is required to have, but you will also appreciate that some of them could be implemented in different ways, requiring some extra effort from your architecture team to decide the best way of doing so.

Here is where the ESB Toolkit comes to help. Based on the years of experience of architects and IT teams building integrations solutions with BizTalk, these patterns and capabilities have been packaged as a set of guidelines and re-usable components that will help you to build an ESB solution with a more predictable and efficient result.

The ESB Toolkit

In this section, we will get to know what the ESB Toolkit is all about, why it was created, and the benefits it brings to any BizTalk solution, especially to build ESB architectures.

We all need a bit of guidance

As we saw in the previous section, ESB is an architectural model that can bring huge benefits to the integration architecture of a company, but there would be potentially many ways to achieve the same goal.

Around 2007, a group of talented architects and developers from the Microsoft BizTalk product group and the Patterns and Practices team came up with the idea of the ESB Guidance, as a set of architectural guidelines and re-usable components that would help us to build an ESB based in Microsoft BizTalk Server 2006 R2. This ESB Guidance was renamed later on to ESB Toolkit with its 2.0 version along with BizTalk 2009. The latest versions of it are the 2.1 that came with BizTalk 2010 (the one that we will cover in this book) and the latest one (2.2) that comes with BizTalk 2013.

The main difference between ESB Toolkit 2.1 and 2.2 versions is that the ESB Toolkit 2.2 can be installed directly from the BizTalk installer splash screen, but the rest remain the same, so the contents described in this book apply to both versions.

Most of the current technologies and IT development platforms nowadays provide huge flexibility and power in terms of implementing solutions, but that flexibility and power sometimes make it difficult to know the better way to implement some common patterns.

In the old days of .NET, we all needed to implement common patterns such as aspect oriented programming, error handling libraries, logging, and so on, and there were teams around the world implementing the same things on and on, each of them on their own flavor. But then the Enterprise Library came along to make our life a bit easier.

The ESB Toolkit is to BizTalk the same as the Enterprise Library is to any .NET application. It just helps to implement common architectural and development practices in a reliable and proven way. Whether you are building an ESB or not, some of the ESB Toolkit principles and re-usable components will be really useful to build high quality BizTalk solutions.

ESB Toolkit features

The aim of the ESB Toolkit is to cover all of the capabilities required by a proper ESB by leveraging existing features in BizTalk Server, introducing new re-usable components and documenting it all together so we don't get lost along the way.

We can map the main ESB capabilities we listed in previous sections to the BizTalk and ESB Toolkit features like:

ESB Capability	Mapping to BizTalk and ESB Toolkit
Message Routing	BizTalk content-based routing and ESB Toolkit itineraries
Connectivity	BizTalk Adapters and ESB Toolkit ramps
Exchange Patterns	BizTalk Adapters and existing architecture
Transformation	BizTalk maps and ESB Toolkit components
Service Directory	BizTalk UDDI Services and ESB Toolkit itineraries
Rules Dynamic Resolution	BizTalk Business Rules and ESB Toolkit dynamic resolution
Validation	BizTalk Schemas and ESB Toolkit components
Aggregation	BizTalk orchestrations and ESB Toolkit itineraries
Service Orchestration	BizTalk orchestrations and ESB Toolkit itineraries
Assured Delivery	BizTalk Adapters and ESB Toolkit Exception Handling
Management and Governance	BizTalk management console, ESB Toolkit management portal, and Business Activity Monitoring (BAM)
Security	BizTalk Security and SSO

As we mentioned earlier, all these capabilities are pretty much required to build a full-blown ESB architecture and they should be interoperable and decoupled enough to provide the flexibility and scalability that we need.

All this can be very well represented with the representation of the ESB Toolkit architecture and main components shown in the following figure.

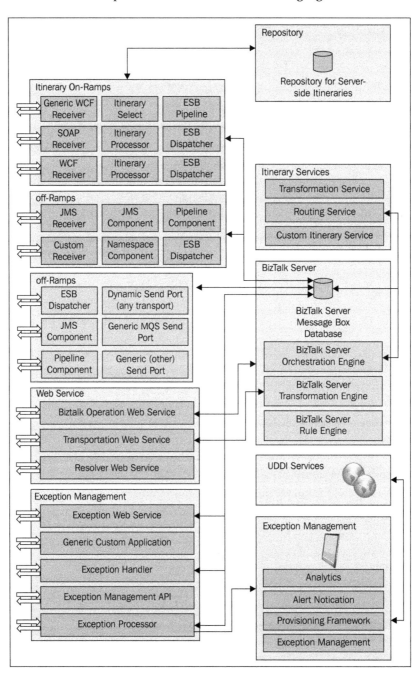

Itineraries

The itinerary is one of the core concepts on the implementation of an ESB solution. It's the definition of the flow of certain piece of information or message must follow, through the ESB to fulfill one specific business process or interface.

The itinerary is composed of a set of steps or processing units that pretty much can be mapped to one or more of the stages defined by the VETRO pattern. Those steps or processing units are called **Itinerary Services**. They can be either the standard itinerary service components that come with the ESB Toolkit (the Transformation and Routing Services) or our own custom developed itinerary services.

We will get to know the itineraries more in detail in the next chapter of this book.

Ramps and web services

The ramps are the connection points where the systems can connect to send messages to the ESB and receive messages from it. Those are respectively the On-Ramps and the Off-Ramps and are implemented as WCF web services and BizTalk send ports, although we could build our own ramps based on other types of BizTalk adapters.

The ESB Toolkit also provides a set of web services that expose the functionality of some ESB features to any external systems. Those services are:

- Itinerary processing
- Exception management
- Endpoints and maps resolution
- Messages transformation
- BizTalk Server operations
- BAM services
- UDDI services

We will cover these in detail in *Chapter 2, Itinerary Services* and *Chapter 4, Understanding the ESB Web Services*.

Services directory

The services directory is provided in BizTalk and the ESB Toolkit by means of the Universal Description, Discovery, and Integration (UDDI) services. These services provide a centralized registry of the services available across an organization, either for internal or external consumers, exposing all of the required information to categorize, organize, discover, and manage those services' definitions.

We will talk more about it in *Chapter 4, Understanding the ESB Web Services*.

Exception Management framework

Exception Management framework is a set of components and APIs that provide a standardized approach to handle, notify, and process any exceptional situations that might occur during the processing of a message. It's pretty much like the counterpart of the exception handling in the Enterprise Library.

We will dedicate a whole chapter to this topic later on in this book.

ESB Management Portal

The ESB Toolkit includes a web portal built on ASP.NET that provides:

- Insight to the status of our ESB processes' health with detailed reporting of any issues that might have happened in any of our ESB applications (with a basic implementation of failed messages reprocessing)

- Alerting features to create notifications for the ESB administrators of any errors that might happen

- Features to manage the new services registry requests users can create

- Different management consoles to configure certain features of the system

We will get into the details of the portal on the last chapter of the book.

 The ESB Management Portal and Service are provided as samples. These will work fine for a development environment.

Other components and utilities

There are many other re-usable components and tools within the ESB Toolkit that are really helpful during the design, development, and operation of our ESB, as well as components that could be easily re-used in other non-ESB implementations, such as certain pipeline components and libraries. One example of those are the Add/ Remove Namespace pipeline components.

Those could come in handy in many BizTalk solutions where we need to deal with systems that are not that careful with how they set the namespaces on the messages submitted to BizTalk. We can use them to:

- Add a namespace when the incoming message doesn't have a root namespace
- Replace the incoming root namespace when the difference between the external system schema and our canonical schemas just differ in their namespace (so we could avoid the implementation and execution of a ridiculously simple map)
- When the type of the inbound message is defined by some data included within the message itself

Summary

In this chapter, we have learned about the main architectural principles that define an Enterprise Service Bus, why the ESB Toolkit was something very much needed to help us to build high quality BizTalk solutions, and what are the main features of the ESB Toolkit.

In the next chapter, we will deep dive on the itineraries concept and how it rules the processing of messages within our ESB.

2
Itinerary Services

As we have discussed in the previous chapter, itineraries are the conceptual definition of the different services and processes that a message should go through to complete a business process within an ESB. Itinerary services are one of the main peculiarities that define how an ESB works. They are the glue that keep many of rest of the features of an ESB together.

In this chapter, we will have a deeper insight into the following:

- What is an itinerary
- What are the itinerary services and their different types
- How to create our own custom itinerary services
- How we stick together our itinerary services within an itinerary
- Deploy and use your itineraries within BizTalk

Decoupling, composing, and evolving

In many aspects of life, complex problems are better solved by breaking down the problem into well-defined smaller problems and solving those smaller problems in a given order. And, even the solution to complex problems that we solved following that decomposition process in the past, might not remain immutable over time.

This is the basic rationale that stands behind the concept of an itinerary.

Any business process can usually be broken down into a set of clearly defined subprocesses. Those subprocesses are usually mapped to specific services or capabilities within an organization (for example, the approval of a specific offer within a purchase order is undertaken by some specific customer care team, the arrangement of the goods shipment is scheduled by the automated delivery system, and so on). All those services have clearly defined duties, and they can carry out their processing in a more or less autonomous/decoupled way. Doesn't it start smelling like SOA?

An ESB itinerary is just the logical representation of how those subprocesses are composed to fulfill the overall business process. The itinerary doesn´t define how each of those processes should implement their duty, but just how the information moves from one subprocess to the other.

Each of those subprocesses will be carried out by what we will call itinerary services. An itinerary service is an autonomous and clearly defined piece of functionality that receives some information or message, does some processing over that information, and in most cases, produces an outcome of that processing.

The autonomous nature of the itinerary services makes it easy to compose different services into an itinerary, and allows them to evolve without having a significant impact on any other services that might be part of that composition.

In the following figure, we can see what could be the three examples of an itinerary that define the overall purchase order management process within an organization, where each of the squares below represent an itinerary service that carries out part of the process:

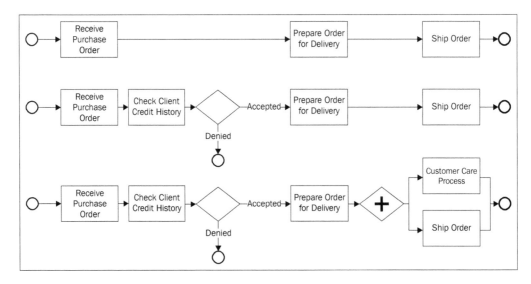

Our initial business process is rather simple, where we have three subprocesses or itinerary services in charge of doing some processing over the specific purchase order.

Over time, as our organization evolves, this business process could evolve and include further subprocesses within the overall process:

- After detecting that some orders where later withdrawn because the client was not able to pay for them, we introduce **Check Client Credit History** in our process.

- As we want to give a better service to our clients, a new customer care process is defined. So after each purchase order, the client is automatically contacted to provide some feedback about our organization.

- Even an existing subprocess might just change instead of being added or removed from the itinerary. We could just engage a new courier services company to deliver our orders.

Thanks to the itinerary-based design of these processes, our business processes can evolve with minimal impact on the rest of the subprocesses involved.

Before we can jump in and start creating itineraries, we must first learn what they are composed of, and how to create them using the tools provided by the BizTalk ESB Toolkit. The following section will provide us with this knowledge.

Itineraries in the BizTalk ESB Toolkit

In this section, we will get into the details of how itineraries are implemented and used specifically in the ESB Toolkit.

Itinerary structure

As we mentioned earlier in this chapter, itineraries are just the representation of the different itinerary services that will be triggered along with the execution of the itinerary itself.

In the initial versions of the ESB Toolkit (when it still was called ESB Guidance), there was really limited tooling to create the actual itinerary definition files, but the Toolkit has evolved providing a nice visual designer that really helps to abstract from those lower-level details of how the itinerary definition file is made up.

There are two main XML structures related to itineraries, as discussed in the following sections.

The itinerary model

The itinerary model is the XML representation that contains all the information required to describe those itinerary services involved in the itinerary. This is the itinerary representation generated at design time by means of the visual Itinerary Designer in Visual Studio. We will have a deeper look into how we work with itinerary models later in the chapter.

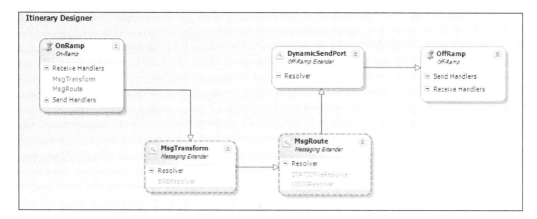

The itinerary metadata instance

This metadata is the actual instance of the itinerary to be applied to a message at runtime. Its structure is defined by the ESB Itinerary Schema (Itinerary.xsd) and its contents are driven by an actual itinerary model.

It travels with the message being processed as part of its context and stores the XML representation of the actual state of the execution of the itinerary. The different itinerary services will retrieve and update it in order to reflect how the itinerary processing progresses.

It has three principal sections:

- ServiceInstance: Represents the current itinerary service that is processing the message.

- Services: Represents the whole set of itinerary services that make up the itinerary. It stores the information about the execution of any previous itinerary services.

- Resolvers: Contains the list of resolvers that will be used by the itinerary services as part of their processing. We will further describe the resolvers' concept later.

The following figure shows an itinerary metadata instance of the itinerary model shown in the previous figure:

```
<?xml version="1.0" encoding="utf-8" ?>
<Itinerary xmlns:xsi="http://www.w3.org/2001/XMLSchema-instance" xmlns:xsd="http://www.w3.org/2001/XMLSchema" uuid="" beginTime=""
  completeTime="" state="Pending" isRequestResponse="false" servicecount="3"
  name="DisassemblerOneWayMessageTransformMessageRoutingMessgeSendPort" version="1.0"
  xmlns="http://schemas.microsoft.biztalk.practices.esb.com/itinerary">
  <BizTalkSegment interchangeId="" epmRRCorrelationToken="" receiveInstanceId="" messageId="" xmlns="" />
  <ServiceInstance name="Microsoft.Practices.ESB.Services.Transform" type="Messaging" state="Pending" position="0" isRequestResponse="false"
    xmlns="" />
  <Services xmlns="">
    <Service uuid="cfbe36c5-d85c-44e9-9549-4a7abf2106c5" beginTime="" completeTime="" name="Microsoft.Practices.ESB.Services.Transform"
      type="Messaging" state="Pending" isRequestResponse="false" position="0" serviceInstanceId="" />
  </Services>
  <Services xmlns="">
    <Service uuid="6a594d80-91f7-4e10-a203-b3c999b0f55e" beginTime="" completeTime="" name="Microsoft.Practices.ESB.Services.Routing"
      type="Messaging" state="Pending" isRequestResponse="false" position="1" serviceInstanceId="" />
  </Services>
  <Services xmlns="">
  <ResolverGroups xmlns="">
    <Resolvers serviceId="Microsoft.Practices.ESB.Services.Transform0"><![CDATA
      [BRE:\\policy=ResolveMap;version=1.0;useMsg=false;messageFile=;recognizeMessageFormat=false;]]></Resolvers>
    <Resolvers serviceId="Microsoft.Practices.ESB.Services.Routing1"><![CDATA
      [STATIC:\\transportType=FILE;transportLocation=C:\Projects\Microsoft.Practices.ESB\Source\Samples\DynamicResolution\Test\Filedrop\OUt\
      %MessageID%.xml;action=;endpointConfig=;jaxRpcResponse=false;messageExchangePattern=;targetNamespace=;transformType=;]]><!
      [CDATA[UDDI3:\\searchQualifiers=andAllKeys;categorySearch=;bindingKey=uddi:esb:orderfileservicev3.1;serviceKey=;]]></Resolvers>
    <Resolvers serviceId="DynamicTest2" />
  </ResolverGroups>
</Itinerary>
```

Working with itinerary models

In order to create an itinerary model, we just need to create a new project of BizTalk ESB Itinerary Designer type, which by default will contain a brand new itinerary model with the .itinerary file extension. We will be able to add as many itinerary models to the project as we need.

The following figure shows the first step we take while creating an itinerary. We start off by selecting the **BizTalk ESB Itinerary Designer** project.

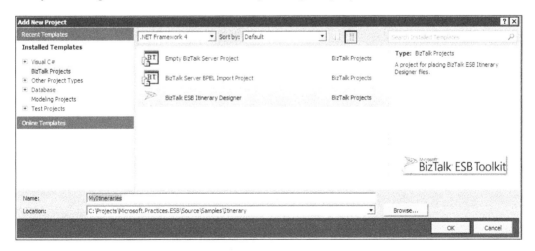

The Itinerary Designer is a **DSL** (**Domain Specific Language**) tool that allows us to drag-and-drop the different model elements that define how our itinerary will behave, connecting those as required, and setting up the corresponding properties.

There are different kinds of elements we can use from the toolbox to build our itinerary model:

- Itinerary services
- On-ramps
- Off-ramps
- Itinerary broker services

Some of these element types have different subtypes that imply different characteristics for them (for example, an itinerary service can be a messaging service, an orchestration service, or an off-ramp extender) and which other elements they can be connected to. This is defined on the Extender property of those elements, as we will see next.

Itinerary services

The itinerary services are components that carry out some processing over the messages flowing through the ESB. The basic processing of an itinerary service is as follows:

1. Receive a message for processing.
2. Process the message.
3. Mark the itinerary step as completed (or failed if something went wrong).
4. Pass the message to the next itinerary service defined in the itinerary definition.

The three types of itinerary services that we can use in the itinerary model are:

- **Messaging services**: These are implemented as components that will run within a pipeline component and execute the message processing during the execution of receive/send pipelines where they are included.
- **Orchestration services**: These are implemented as orchestrations.
- **Off-ramp extenders**: These don't necessarily do any processing, but define in the itinerary model that the next service to execute is an off-ramp.

One key ESB Toolkit concept that concerns itinerary services is the Resolution framework that we will explain later in this chapter.

On-ramps

The itinerary on-ramp is a logical representation of the receive port that will initiate the itinerary execution. An itinerary mode can contain only one on-ramp.

The only extender type this element supports is the `On-Ramp ESB Extender`. This extender type has two more properties associated with it that we have to define in order to link the on-ramp with the receive port that will effectively receive the messages to be processed by the itinerary:

- `BizTalk Application`: Here, we will set the name of the BizTalk application to where the receive port is contained.

- `Receive Port`: Here, we will set the name of the port to be associated with the on-ramp.

 The ESB Toolkit already includes two itinerary receiver ports (for both one way and request/response itineraries execution) that cover all the standard ESB message reception scenarios, so we shouldn't need to create our own itinerary receive ports and just use those already defined in the **Microsoft.Practices.ESB** BizTalk application.

On-ramp is also a logical container that defines the different itinerary services that will process the corresponding message on its way in (**Receive Handlers**) or on its way out (**Send Handlers** in case we are talking of a request/response on-ramp). The Receive and Send handlers effectively represent where the messaging itinerary services will be executed, either on the way in or in the way out of the ramp. We will describe further the messaging itinerary services later in the *Itinerary Services* section.

Off-ramps

The itinerary off-ramp is a logical representation of the send port that will send out a message from the ESB as part of the itinerary execution. An itinerary model can contain one or more off-ramps.

The only extender type this element supports is the `Off-Ramp ESB Extender`. This extender type has two more properties associated with it that we have to define in order to link the off-ramp with the send port that will effectively send the messages to the target system:

- `BizTalk Application`: Here, we will set the name of the BizTalk application where the send port is contained.

- `Send Port`: Here, we will set the name of the port to be associated with off-ramp.

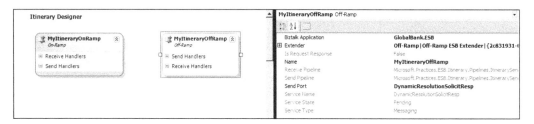

The send ports that are associated with the off-ramp need to be configured with the appropriate subscription filters, so that they receive the messages they should process. The filter required on an itinerary service is made up of at least three different elements that are the BizTalk message context properties it will filter on:

- The `Microsoft.Practices.ESB.Itinerary.Schemas.ServiceName` property has a value that is the name of the service the port provides.

- The `Microsoft.Practices.ESB.Itinerary.Schemas.ServiceState` property value is `Pending`, indicating the current itinerary step the message should be processed by is pending.

- The `Microsoft.Practices.ESB.Itinerary.Schemas.ServiceType` property value is `Messaging`, indicating that the service that should process the message is a messaging service and not an orchestration (we could have the save itinerary service implemented as a messaging and orchestration service)

A port that is meant to be used to run an itinerary service should be a dynamic port, so it supports the execution of dynamic end point resolution provided by the routing itinerary service that comes out-of-the-box with the ESB Toolkit. This itinerary service is explained later in the chapter.

The same way as on-ramp, off-ramp is a logical container that defines the different itinerary services that will process the corresponding message on its way out (**Send Handlers**) or on its way in (**Receive Handlers** in case we are talking of a request/response off-ramp). These handlers will also be messaging itinerary services within the send and receive pipelines of the port.

Resolution framework

The ESB Toolkit Resolution framework is intended to dynamically resolve processing information within the ESB. This adds an extra indirection level in the ESB processing by providing a decoupled manner of directing how information is processed by the ESB, without needing to modify the actual implementation of an ESB process.

An ESB Resolver is responsible of taking some input information (either contained in the resolver connection string or in the message being processed itself), and produce a set of results that can be used downstream to guide the processing of the message. The result of the resolver is called Resolver Dictionary that is just a set of name/ value pairs that contain different properties derived from the resolution process. Those name/value pairs can be used by downstream components (like itinerary services or adapters) to dynamically set context properties on the message being processed, or take decisions on how to continue processing the message.

The resolver connection string is made up of two main pieces:

- **Moniker**: Moniker defines the actual type of resolver that will be invoked to do the resolution.
- **Connection properties**: They are a set of name/value pairs that the resolver uses as an input for the resolution process.

The full resolver connection string would look like the following line:

```
{moniker}:\\{property name}={property value};
{property name}={property value}
```

The resolvers included by default in the ESB Toolkit are (listed using their corresponding monikers):

- STATIC: The results of the resolution are directly defined in the resolver connection string. It's mainly used for endpoint and transformation information resolution. The main properties used with this resolver are:
    - ○ TransportType: Defines the transport/adapter that will be used to communicate with the target endpoint (for example, FILE, FTP, SMTP, MQSeries, WCF-BasicHttp, WCF-WSHttpor WCF-Custom).
    - ○ TransportLocation: Specifies the actual address of the target endpoint (for example, web service URL)
    - ○ Action: The action/operation meant to handle the request on the target endpoint (for example, the SOAP action in the target web service).

- ○ `EndpointConfig`: Sets additional configuration properties for the corresponding adapter. It's a name/value pair's list that contains properties that can be used to further configure certain adapters. We can see the whole list of `EndpointConfig` elements that can be used by opening the corresponding Endpoint Configuration property in the resolver (the list depends on the `TransportType` value). For example, we can see the list of endpoint properties for the WCF-BasicHttp transport in the following screenshot:

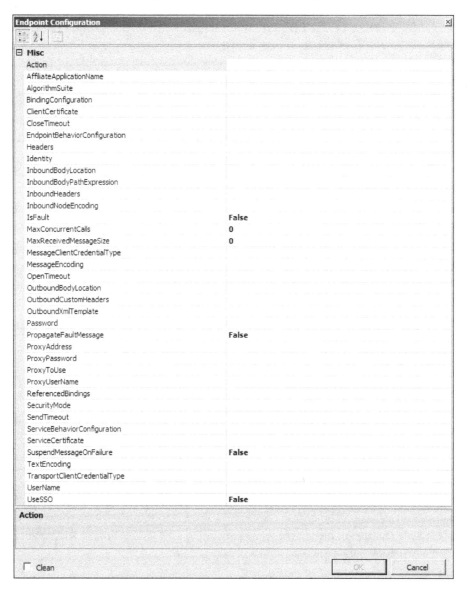

- ○ `TargetNamespace`: The actual namespace to be used on messages sent to the target endpoint.

- ○ `TransformType`: The fully qualified name of the type that implements the transformation that should be applied to the outbound message.

- `UDDI`: The results of the resolution are taken by querying a UDDI registry whose URL is defined in the connection string. The properties used in the connection string define how UDDI should be queried:

    - ○ `ServerUrl`: Defines the URL of the UDDI server to query.

    - ○ `ServiceName`: Defines the name of the service registered in UDDI that contains the information to be returned as a result of the resolution.

    - ○ `ServiceProvider`: Defines the name of the service provider the service we want to resolve is associated with in UDDI.

- `XPATH`: Each result of the resolution is taken from the contents of the inbound message by means of XPATH queries. For example, we could set the `TransportLocation` property to be extracted from certain node in the message XML by means of the corresponding XPATH query (`TransportLocation=/*[local-name()='OrderDoc' and namespace-uri()='http://globalbank.esb.dynamicresolution.com/northamericanservices/']/*[local-name()='ID' and namespace-uri()='http://globalbank.esb.dynamicresolution.com/northamericanservices/'];`).

- `BRE`: The results of the resolution, and produced by means of the execution of a BizTalk Rule Engine policy. The properties set in the connection string define which policy should be executed:

    - ○ `Policy`: Defines the name of the policy that should be executed.

    - ○ `Version`: Defines the version of the policy meant to be executed.

    - ○ `UseMesage`: Defines if the message is provided to the policy as an input fact to be used during the execution of the policy.

- `BRI`: Similar to BRE, but used to resolve (through a business rule) the itinerary name and version to be applied on a message, by means of the `ESB.Itinerary` vocabulary. The properties in the connection string are the same as in the BRE resolver.

- ITINERARY and ITINERARY-STATIC: Used to resolve the itinerary to be used to process a message, retrieving it from the itinerary repository as instructed by the name and version defined on the connection string. Both the resolvers use the same connection string properties:
    ○ Name: Name of the itinerary.
    ○ Version: Version of the itinerary.

- LDAP: Retrieves information from Active Directory objects to populate the resolution results. The connection string properties specify both how the active directory should be queried (for example, filter to be applied to the query), as well as from which properties in the active directory object returned by the LDAP query should be used to retrieve resolution values (for example, with TransportLocation={mail} we declare that the transport location should be retrieved from the value of the mail property of the active directory object).

We can even create our own resolvers to implement any other type of custom resolution we might need.

Now, we will look in detail into the different choices that we have when we add an itinerary service shape into our model.

Messaging itinerary services

This type of itinerary service is basically classes that do some processing on the message during the execution of a pipeline.

These components are executed as instructed by the itinerary model by a pipeline component within a specific pipeline that will be used as a receive or send pipeline in a port, so while the message travels through the pipeline, each of these components will receive the message, do some processing on it if required, and hand it over to the next component (or to the message box / corresponding adapter in case it's the last component of the receive/send pipeline).

The ESB Toolkit includes two pipeline components (ESB Dispatcher and ESB Dispatcher Disassembler) that both take care of executing messaging itinerary services registered in the ESB. There are two services that come with the ESB Toolkit:

- **Routing service**: Used to resolve and apply routing information to the message. Basically resolves and applies the context properties required to route the message to one specific endpoint or send port. It can route the same message to multiple endpoints, by using multiple resolvers (each resolver execution will represent the message being sent to a different endpoint).

- **Mapping service**: Used to dynamically resolve and apply a map into the message being processed.

You can use these components in your own pipelines, but the ESB Toolkit already includes a series of send and receive pipelines that use those components. Those pipelines are in turn used on the different ports that build up the basic artifacts of the ESB Toolkit (for example, default on-ramp itinerary receive ports) or can be used in our own send and receive ports. There are other pipeline components that can be included in those pipelines that are not really itinerary services, but are involved in the itinerary processing framework itself, or support some other features of the ESB Toolkit. We will list those later in this chapter.

The messaging itinerary services have the benefit that they are quicker to execute (reducing latency) and less resource-intensive than the orchestration-based itinerary services.

To add one of these into the itinerary in the itinerary model designer, you will just drag-and-drop an itinerary service shape and set the **Itinerary Service Extender** type to `Messaging`. You will also select the itinerary service that will be actually executed. As you can see, by default we just see the two services that come with the ESB Toolkit:

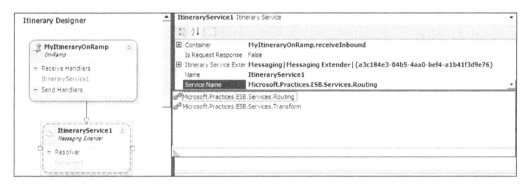

By setting the `Container` property in the shape properties we will be able to define if the service is meant to be executed in the way in of the ramp (**Receive Handlers**) or in the way out of the ramp (**Send Handlers**). You will notice that the shape border changes a little bit from one value to the other (a dashed border for **Receiver Handlers** and a dotted border for the **Send Handlers**).

You can also add a resolver to the itinerary service. This one will be used to actually resolve information required to execute the service (for example, resolve the map to be applied to the message).

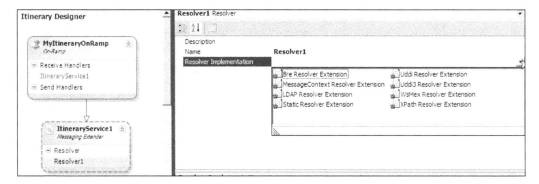

Orchestration itinerary services

These types of itinerary services are implemented within a BizTalk orchestration. They follow the same basic process of a messaging itinerary service, but the difference is that they hand over the message for further processing by any downstream itinerary service by means of ports:

1. Receive the message.
2. Retrieve the current itinerary status.
3. Do some processing.
4. Advance the itinerary to the next step.
5. Send the message.

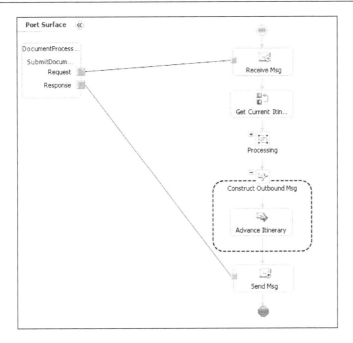

The ESB Toolkit provides two out-of-the-box orchestration itinerary services that are the counterparts of the ones provided in the messaging flavor:

- **Delivery service**: Used to resolve and apply routing information to the message.
- **Transform service**: Used to dynamically resolve and apply a map into the message being processed.

You can also implement your own orchestration services just by following the same processing pattern we just discussed.

The orchestration itinerary services add some processing overhead intrinsic to the orchestration execution lifecycle, but have the benefit of being more flexible in terms of composition, and allow us to implement more complex itineraries and itinerary services.

In the Itinerary Designer, you will just drop an itinerary service shape as we did before, but this time we will choose `Orchestration` on the `Itinerary Service Extender` property. The same way, we will choose the service that will process this itinerary step from those orchestrations that implement itinerary services.

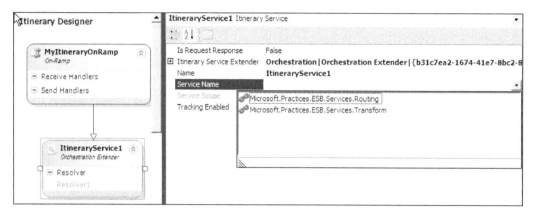

Off-ramp extenders

This variant of the itinerary service shape is a peculiar one because these don't actually execute any processing on the message. They are just required by design to define the stage where an off-ramp will be executed as the next step of the process, and so any messaging itinerary services executed within the off-ramp send port pipeline will run.

As we can see in the following screenshot, it just precedes the off-ramp and the messaging service to be executed on the way out of the message:

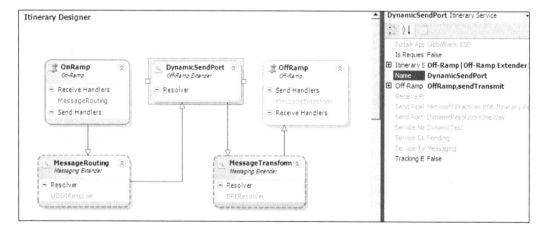

Other itinerary components

As we mentioned before, the ESB Toolkit provides a series of pipeline components that either support the execution of itineraries or add extra features to be executed while a message travels through the itinerary, but are not itinerary services as such:

- **ESB Itinerary Selector**: You can use this component on the receive side (in a receive pipeline) to select a server-side itinerary for a message to follow. This component can be configured with a resolver connection string, which will be the one used to trigger the corresponding resolver and retrieve the name of the itinerary to apply to the message.

- **ESB Itinerary**: You can use this component on the receive side (in a receive pipeline) to promote ESB metadata properties from SOAP headers into the message context. In this case, the client that submits the message for processing, attaches the itinerary metadata into the web service calls to the itinerary web services, and so this component extracts that data from the inbound web service call.

- **ESB Itinerary Forwarder**: This component can be used on the send pipeline of a two-way send port to be able to invoke two or more web service calls sequentially on an itinerary, without needing to put an orchestration service between them. This component makes the required changes into the message context to make the response message from a two-way port execution be routed to the next web service call, instead of being directly delivered as a response to the initiating receive port.

- **ESB Itinerary Cache**: You can use this component to cache itineraries and reapply them to response messages received in solicit-response send ports.

- **ESB JMS Decoder**: You can use this component on the receive side (in a receive location) of an orchestration or a send port to parse out IBM JMS (MQRFH2) headers and preserve them as context properties. You can then access these context properties and modify them in the same way as any other BizTalk context properties.

- **ESB JMS Encoder**: You can use this component in a send port to write IBM JMS (MQRFH2) headers to messages.

- **ESB Add Namespace**: You can use this component in either a receive location or a send port to add namespaces to XML documents.

- **ESB Remove Namespace**: You can use this component in either a receive location or a send port to remove namespaces from XML documents.

- **ESB Exception Encoder**: You can use this component to send fault messages to the file system, Microsoft InfoPath, or Microsoft SharePoint. This component is part of the ESB exception handling mechanism, and it normalizes and enriches all exceptions processed by a send port. The component serializes exception information (including embedded persisted messages and context properties) into a canonical format so that all contained messages and the exception itself are available.

- **ESB BAM Tracker**: You can use this component to intercept the fault message emitted from the ESB Exception Encoder and insert the data in the message into the BAM Primary Import table (using the BAM Event Stream in the pipeline). This component is part of the ESB exception handling mechanism.

Itinerary broker services

This is the last type of shape that we can add into our itineraries. It's meant to allow us to make decisions on which should be the next itinerary service to execute, so they are some sort of if/switch clause in terms of programming languages.

This shape comes together with another shape, the itinerary broker outport. This is the one that will link the itinerary broker service shape to each of the possible routes the message could take as a next step in the itinerary.

The process to set up a broker service is as follows:

1. We will add the broker service into the design surface.

2. We will drop one outport into the broker service for each of those routes the message could follow.

3. We will define one or more resolvers that will be used to retrieve the information that will be used as the input to decide the next step the message should take.

4. We will define one or more filters (at least one for each of the outports to be added) that will be the logical decisions that will be applied to the resolvers' outcome to decide if the message should follow the corresponding outport or not.

5. We will drop one outport shape into the broker service shape for each of the routes the message could follow.

6. For each of those outports, we will associate them with one resolver and one filter. That combination will be the one that will cause the outport to be followed or not at runtime.

In the following example, we see that we created two outports in the broker service, both of them using the same resolver, but each of them with their own filter.

We could just set the type of the resolver used to CONTEXT (this one will return as a result of the resolution the collection of context properties of the message) and set filters' expressions to:

- `GoToService1: //Property[@name='InboundTransportType']='FILE'`
- `GoToService2: //Property[@name='InboundTransportType']!='FILE'`

The message would then just be delivered to the corresponding next itinerary service, depending on if it was received from a file port or not.

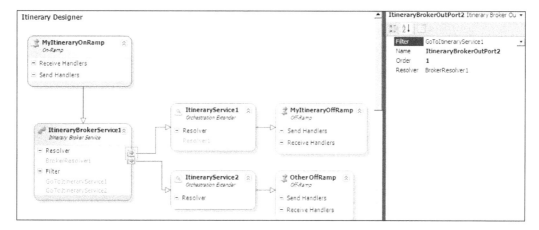

The finishing touch

We went through the main components that build up an itinerary, but to finish it off we need to put them together and look into some other properties we can set in there.

Itinerary properties

If you click on the design surface outside of any shape, you'll see in the properties pane the properties of the itinerary itself:

- **BizTalk Server Connection String**: It defines the BizTalk database from which the model designer can identify where to look up the artifacts available so on that you can select those while designing your itinerary (for example, business rules for your resolvers).

- **Encryption Certificate**: You can select a certificate that will be used to encrypt any sensitive data in your itinerary definition (for example, passwords).

- **Require Encryption Certificate**: It enables or disables the requirement to have an encryption certificate defined.

- **Is Request Response**: Basically, specifies if the itinerary will be two-way, so it will generate some output to be sent as a response through the inbound on-ramp that in such cases should be defined as request/response as well.

- **Name**: The name that will identify the itinerary.

- **Version**: The version of the itinerary.

- **Resolver Service URL**: The resolver service URL that will be used to test the resolver configuration.

- **Model Exporter**: It defines how the itinerary model will be exported for later use. It can be:

    ○ **XML Exporter**: The model will be exported into an XML file.

    ○ **Database Exporter**: The model will be exported into XML, but will be published directly into the itinerary database.

We can see these properties in the following screenshot:

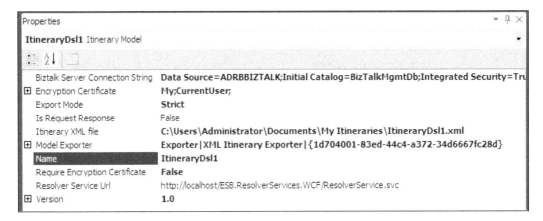

Itinerary services tracking

Each itinerary service shape that you drop into the design surface has a `Tracking Enabled` property. When it´s set to true, every time that itinerary service is executed, it´s execution will be traced into BAM, so we will be able to create views and reports on the execution of our itineraries.

As you might have noticed, there's an additional element in the itinerary designer toolbox — the connector. What will it be used for?

Yes, the connector is just meant to link the itinerary model elements to each other.

Deploying our itineraries

In order to make our itineraries available on the ESB to be used (and more importantly resolved by the components mentioned before), they need to be published into the ESB.

They need to be published into the `ESBItinerary` database that is created during the installation of the ESB toolkit. That database has a single table that contains all the details of the itineraries, like their name, their version, and the XML representation of their model.

We can deploy them directly from Visual Studio, by using the **Database Exporter** mentioned in the itinerary properties section. We just need to right-click on the design surface, and then click on **Export Model**.

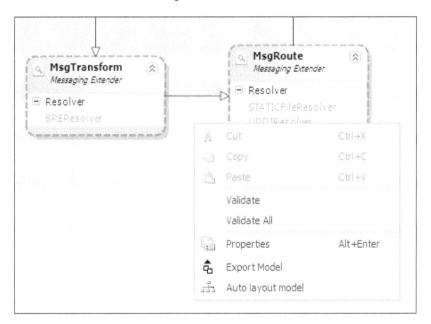

In case we export our models into XML files, we can import them later into the itineraries database by using a small tool provided with the ESB Toolkit. You can find the `ESBImportUtil.exe` tool in the following folder:

```
C:\Program Files (x86)\Microsoft BizTalk ESB Toolkit 2.1\Bin
```

```
Administrator: C:\Windows\system32\cmd.exe                              _ □ X
Microsoft Windows [Version 6.1.7601]
Copyright (c) 2009 Microsoft Corporation.  All rights reserved.

C:\Users\Administrator>"C:\Program Files (x86)\Microsoft BizTalk ESB Toolkit 2.1
\Bin\EsbImportUtil.exe"
Syntax:

/?: <Show the parameters help>
/f: <Itinerary xml file path>
/c: <published | deployed>
/n: <Default Itinerary name>
/v: <Default Itinerary version (format 'mayor.minor')>
/o  <Silent overwrite>

Publish to Itinerary DB: esbimportutil.exe /f:myitinerary.xml /c:published
Deploy to Itinerary DB: esbimportutil.exe  /f:myitinerary.xml /c:deployed

C:\Users\Administrator>
```

The arguments for the tool are quite self-explanatory, but there's one that is worth mentioning. It's the itinerary status (`/c:` argument in the previous screenshot). It has two possible values:

- `Published`: The itinerary is just imported with the published status but not deployed, so it won't be available to be used right away. This will allow you to enable or disable the itinerary later on the management portal without removing the itinerary record from the database.

- `Deployed`: The itinerary is imported directly in the deployed status, so it can start being used right away.

You can also set the value of this argument in Visual Studio when you use the **Database Exporter**.

Creating custom itinerary services

In this section, we will see how to create our own custom itinerary services, both on their messaging and orchestration flavors.

Custom messaging itinerary service

As we mentioned before, the messaging services are implemented as specific classes that will be invoked by the ESB Dispatcher pipeline components.

In order to implement one of those, we need to create a class that implements the `IMessagingService` interface. This interface defines two properties (`Name` and `SupportsDisassemble`) and two methods (`Execute` and `ShouldAdvanceStep`) that have to be implemented:

- `Name`: It is the name of the service that will be used to reference the service in the itinerary. It will be the one that will identify the service once registered in the ESB configuration file.

- `SupportsDisassemble`: It specifies if the component supports disassemble and the execution of multiple resolvers.

- `Execute`: It is the method where the processing of the message will take place.

- `ShouldAdvanceStep`: It instructs the Dispatcher to advance the itinerary to the next step or not once the component has finalized its processing.

We will now show the implementation of the `Execute` method for an itinerary service that will perform some compression logic on the body of the message if the resolver used by the service says so:

```
publicMicrosoft.BizTalk.Message.Interop.IBaseMessage
Execute(Microsoft.BizTalk.Component.Interop.IPipelineContext
context, Microsoft.BizTalk.Message.Interop.IBaseMessage msg, string
resolverString, IItineraryStep step)
        {
if (context == null)
thrownewArgumentNullException("context");
if (msg == null)
thrownewArgumentNullException("msg");
if (string.IsNullOrEmpty(resolverString))
thrownewArgumentException(Properties.Resources.ArgumentStringRequired,
"resolverString");

ResolverInfo info = ResolverMgr.GetResolverInfo(ResolutionType.
Endpoint, resolverString);
if (!info.Success)
thrownewException(Properties.Resources.ResolverStringInvalid,
resolverString);


//Resolve if the message is meant to be compressed
```

```
Dictionary<string, string> resolverDictionary = ResolverMgr.
Resolve(info, msg, context);


if (!string.IsNullOrEmpty(resolverDictionary["Acme.
RequiresCompression"]))
            {

IBaseMessagePart bodyPart = msg.BodyPart;
string tmpString = "";
if (bodyPart != null)
                {
try
                {
                        System.IO.StreamReader sr = newSystem.
IO.StreamReader(bodyPart.Data);

tmpString = sr.ReadToEnd();

tmpString = Acme.CompressContent(tmpString);

                        System.IO.MemoryStream strm = newSystem.
IO.MemoryStream(ASCIIEncoding.Default.GetBytes(tmpString));
                        strm.Position = 0;
                        bodyPart.Data = strm;
context.ResourceTracker.AddResource(strm);
                    }
catch (System.Exception ex)
                    {
throw ex;

                    }
                }
            }
return msg;
            }
```

Our resolver could be any kind of resolver that returns the `RequiresCompression` items as part of its resolution result. For example, it could be a business rule that depending on certain properties of the message decides if the message is to be compressed or not.

Once our custom itinerary service is compiled, we will need to deploy it to our BizTalk environment:

- We will deploy it into the GAC of each of the BizTalk servers that compose our environment.

- In the `ESB.Config` file (located in the ESB Toolkit installation path), we will add a new `itineraryService` entry on the `ItineraryServices` section, being its attributes:

    ○ `ID`: A guide for the service.

    ○ `Name`: The name returned by the `Name` property of the component implemented.

    ○ `Type`: The fully qualified name of the class that implements the service.

    ○ `Scope`: It must be `Messaging`, as this is a messaging service.

    ○ `Stage`: The stages of an itinerary where the service can run. It can be `OnRampReceive`, `OnRampSend`, `OffRampSend`, `OffRampReceive`, `AllSend`, `AllReceive`, or `All`.

The following screenshot is an example of the `ESB.Config` file:

```xml
<?xml version="1.0" encoding="utf-8"?>
<!--
    ESB configuration file mapped using File provider
    Used as alternative to SSO configuration
-->
<configuration>
    <configSections>...</configSections>
    <connectionStrings>...</connectionStrings>
    <!-- ESB configuration section -->

    <esb>
        <!-- validation settings used to validate the encryption X509 Certificate -->
        <x509CertificateAuthentication certificateValidationMode="ChainTrust" revocationMode="Online" />
        <bizTalkInformation schemeAssembly="Microsoft.BizTalk.GlobalPropertySchemas, Version=3.0.1.0, Culture=neutral, PublicKeyToken=31b
        <adapterMgr cacheManager="Adapter Cache Manager" absoluteExpiration="3600" />
        <itineraryPipelineCache cacheManager="Itinerary Pipeline Cache Manager" absoluteExpiration="3600" />
        <resolvers cacheManager="Resolver Provid" absoluteExpiration="3600">...</resolvers>
        <adapterProviders cacheManager="Adapter Provider" absoluteExpiration="3600">...</adapterProviders>
        <itineraryServices cacheManager="Itinerary Services Cache Manager" absoluteExpiration="3600">
            <itineraryService id="6a594d80-91f7-4e10-a203-b3c999b0f55e" name="Microsoft.Practices.ESB.Services.Routing" type="Microsoft.Pra
            stage="AllReceive"/>
            <itineraryService id="774488bc-e5b9-4a4e-9ae7-d25cdf23fd1c" name="Microsoft.Practices.ESB.Services.Routing" type="Microsoft.Pra
            stage="None"/>
            <itineraryService id="cfbe36c5-d85c-44e9-9549-4a7abf2106c5" name="Microsoft.Practices.ESB.Services.Transform" type="Microsoft.P
            stage="All" />
            <itineraryService id="92d3b293-e6d4-44a1-b27d-c42b48aec667" name="Microsoft.Practices.ESB.Services.Transform" type="Microsoft.P
            stage="None"/>
            <itineraryService id="977f085f-9f6d-4c18-966f-90bed114f649" name="Microsoft.Practices.ESB.Services.SendPort" type="Microsoft.Pr
            stage="AllReceive" />
            <itineraryService id="4810569C-8FF2-4162-86CE-47692A0B4017" name="Microsoft.Practices.ESB.Itinerary.Services.Broker.MessagingBr
        </itineraryServices>
        <filters cacheManager="Filter Cache Manager" absoluteExpiration="3600">
            <filter name="XPATH" type="Microsoft.Practices.ESB.Filters.XPath.XPathFilter, Microsoft.Practices.ESB.Filters.XPath, Version=2.
```

Custom orchestration itinerary service

Now we will create the same compression service that we created in the previous section, but in the orchestration itinerary service flavor.

The message processing lifecycle of this type of services is pretty much the same as in the messaging services (receive, process, mark step as complete, and send) but with slight differences. Let's start designing our orchestration, and we will highlight those differences as we move on.

Receiving the message

In the messaging services, the message is received by the Dispatcher pipeline component as the message flows through the pipeline, but the orchestration services receive them from the BizTalk message box, and so it'll need to subscribe to the messages they are meant to process. The orchestration will subscribe to those messages that match the following context properties filter:

- The `Microsoft.Practices.ESB.Itinerary.Schemas.ServiceName` property has a value that is the name of the service implemented by the orchestration.

- The `Microsoft.Practices.ESB.Itinerary.Schemas.ServiceState` property value is `Pending`.

- The `Microsoft.Practices.ESB.Itinerary.Schemas.ServiceType` property value is `Orchestration`.

We will drop our port shape into the orchestration design surface. The port name, port type name, and operation names should follow the naming conventions established in your solution for this type of artifact (and should be consistent across the different itinerary services you implement). We will use a direct port binding, as we will receive the messages by means of the specific filters just mentioned.

The port can be either one way or request/response (depending on our service design). The only differences if we use a request/response are:

- Our itinerary service will need to be defined as request/response in our itineraries (and so the itinerary should be request/response as well).

- When we get to the point to deliver the response message, we will need to initialize one extra correlation set to initialize the context properties that will make the message to be routed back directly to the request/response port that initially received the message.

We will now create the inbound and outbound messages for our orchestration. The type of messages sent and received by our orchestration itinerary services will be always of `System.Xml.XmlDocument` type.

Once we have the port and the messages created, we will add the corresponding receive shape. The receive shape will receive the inbound message that we just created. Finally, we will set up the receive shape filter as described previously, and connect it to the receive operation of the receive port.

 Obviously, the `Activate` property of the receive shape will need to be set to `true`.

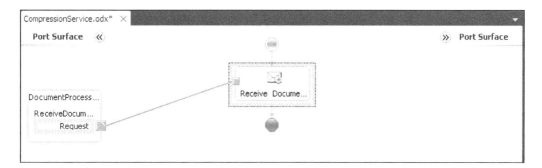

Processing the message

The processing of the message within the orchestration has three principal steps: retrieve the current itinerary state, executing the actual service process, and advancing the itinerary to the next step.

Retrieving itinerary state

This process will give us access to the current state of the itinerary (stored in the message context) the message is flowing through and to the current itinerary step itself.

The most important information that we will be able to retrieve from the itinerary step are the resolvers that are configured for that step in the itinerary, in order to execute them (if necessary) for our later processing.

Firstly, we will create the variables that we need to store the information to be retrieved from the itinerary:

- `itinerary`: It is the variable of `Microsoft.Practices.ESB.Itinerary. SerializableItineraryWrapper` type that will be assigned the itinerary metadata.

- `itineraryStep`: It is the variable of `Microsoft.Practices.ESB. Itinerary.SerializableItineraryStepWrapper` type that will be assigned the current itinerary step information.

- `resolverDictionary`: It is the variable of `Microsoft.Practices.ESB. Resolver.ResolverDictionary` type that will store the results from the resolution.

Once we have our variables defined, we will drop an expression shape into the design surface, as you can see in the following image. In that expression shape, we will retrieve the itinerary metadata, the resolvers for the current itinerary step, and then, we will execute the resolution.

```
//Instantiate the itinerary and itineraryStep classes that will
be used to hold the itinerary the message is going through and the
current itinerary step
itinerary = new Microsoft.Practices.ESB.Itinerary.
SerializableItineraryWrapper();
itineraryStep = new Microsoft.Practices.ESB.Itinerary.
SerializableItineraryStepWrapper();

itinerary.Itinerary = Microsoft.Practices.ESB.Itinerary.
ItineraryOMFactory.Create(InboundMessage);
itineraryStep.ItineraryStep = itinerary.Itinerary.GetItineraryStep(In
boundMessage);
```

```
//Execute the resolver this service is meant to use to resolve the
information that might drive the execution of the service
resolverDictionary = Microsoft.Practices.ESB.Resolver.
ResolverMgr.Resolve(OutboundMessage, itineraryStep.ItineraryStep.
ResolverCollection[0]);

System.Diagnostics.Trace.WriteLine("ServiceName: " + itineraryStep.
ItineraryStep.ServiceName);
System.Diagnostics.Trace.WriteLine("ServiceType: " + System.Convert.
ToString(itineraryStep.ItineraryStep.ServiceType));
```

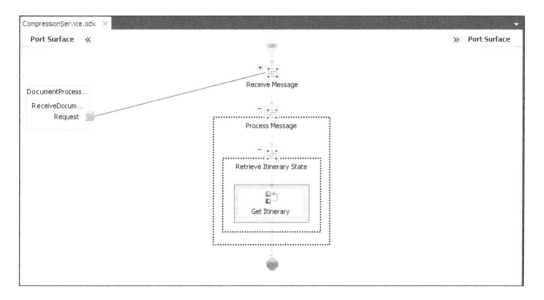

Actual processing

Next, we will add a decision shape. Depending on the resolution result that tells us to execute the compression or not, we will construct the outbound message with the compressed inbound message, or with the unmodified inbound message.

We will use the following sentence in the `Yes` branch of the decision shape:

```
!System.String.IsNullOrEmpty(resolverDictionary.Item("Acme.
RequiresCompression"))
```

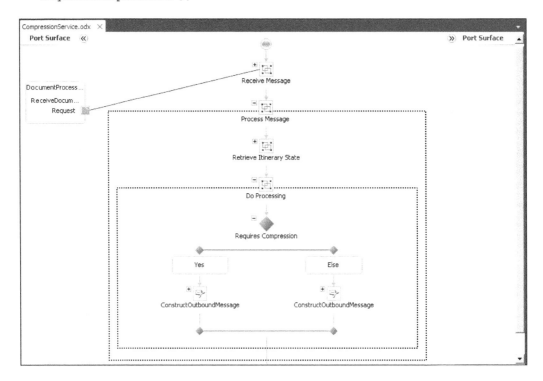

Completing the itinerary step

In order to let the message be processed by downstream services, we need to mark the current itinerary step as completed. Otherwise, when the message is published back into the message box, our orchestration will continue picking up and processing the message in an infinite loop.

We just need an additional expression shape to execute the corresponding itinerary helper classes that will do the magic.

```
System.Diagnostics.Trace.WriteLine("          BEGIN - Advance
Itinerary");

// Call the Itinerary helper to advance to the next step
itinerary.Itinerary.Advance(OutboundMessage, itineraryStep.
ItineraryStep);
itinerary.Itinerary.Write(OutboundMessage);
```

```
System.Diagnostics.Trace.WriteLine("          FINISH - Advance
Itinerary");
```

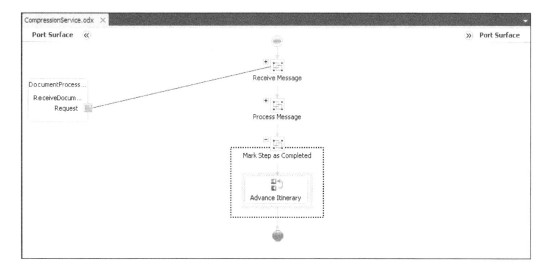

Sending the message

Finally, we will send the outbound message on its way back to the message box for further processing.

We will create a direct binding send port and the corresponding send shape. Additionally, we will create a correlation set and its corresponding correlation set type, which will be initialized in the send shape to promote the context properties needed for itinerary processing. We will name the correlation set type as itineraryAdvance and the correlation properties will be:

- Microsoft.Practices.ESB.Itinerary.Schemas.IsRequestResponse
- Microsoft.Practices.ESB.Itinerary.Schemas.ServiceName
- Microsoft.Practices.ESB.Itinerary.Schemas.ServiceState
- Microsoft.Practices.ESB.Itinerary.Schemas.ServiceType

In case our service is a request/response one, we will need an additional correlation set and correlation set type to promote the context properties that will make the message routed to the request/response port that originally received the initial message. The correlation set type name will be `itineraryRequestResponse` and the correlation properties will be:

- `BTS.CorrelationToken`

- `BTS.EpmRRCorrelationToken`

- `BTS.IsRequestResponse`

- `BTS.ReqRespTransmitPipelineID`

- `BTS.RouteDirectToTP`

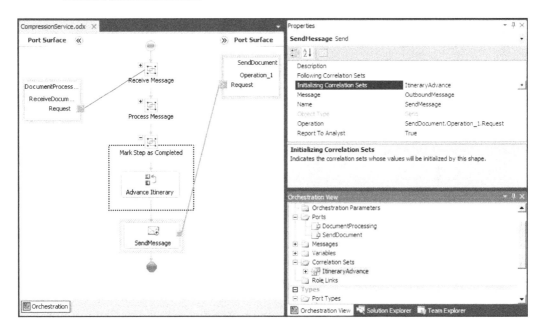

Registering the itinerary service

Before we can use the service in our itineraries, we need to register it on the ESB like we did with the messaging service. The only difference is that the service `Scope` property value will be `Orchestration`.

Executing itineraries

There are multiple ways of executing or invoking our itineraries, where the message sender provides explicitly more or less information about the itinerary to execute:

- **Submitting the message through the ESB Itinerary Web Services**: The client sends the message invoking those web services and attaching to the request a SOAP header that contains the actual itinerary to execute. In this scenario, the initiator has full control and responsibility over what steps compose the itinerary. We will know more about this on the chapter dedicated to the ESB Web Services.

- **Using the Itinerary Selector pipeline component with dynamic resolution**: The message is received through a port whose receive pipeline uses the Itinerary Selector, configured with a resolver connection string that will find out the itinerary to apply (for example, a BRI resolver connection string). In this scenario, the consumer has relative control over the selection of the itinerary, as some information provided by the consumer could be used as an input for the resolution, and so could influence on its result.

- **Using the Itinerary Selector pipeline component with static resolution**: The same component is used, but in this case we use a resolver that statically defines the itinerary that will be executed (for example; an ITINERARY connection string). Here, the name of the itinerary and its version is defined in the configuration of the pipeline component, so the consumer has no control at all to select the itinerary that will be executed.

Summary

In this chapter, we have learned all about itineraries: how they work, how are they built, and how we can extend them and use them in our solutions.

In the next chapter, we will learn how the ESB Toolkit helps us to deal with those situations where things go wrong, so we will learn all about exception management in our ESB.

3
ESB Exception Handling

Being prepared for situations when something goes wrong is always a key concept for the design and implementation of any IT solution. Depending on the scenario, we will need to decide whether to implement proactive or reactive error handling and how to handle system exceptions in opposition to a functional exception scenario.

 It's always advisable to re-use existing and proven frameworks or components instead of reinventing the wheel.

In this chapter, we will explore the benefits provided by the ESB Exception Handling framework:

- The artifacts and patterns for exception handling included in the ESB Toolkit
- How to capture and publish exceptions
- How to monitor exceptions in the ESB Management Portal
- How to repair and resubmit messages into the ESB

Error handling in BizTalk and the ESB Toolkit

The ESB Toolkit Exception Handling framework is meant to complement and standardize the usage of the existing error handling features included in BizTalk. The out of the box error handling features included in BizTalk are good, but a support model based solely on these becomes too manual and laborious for the teams supporting the solution. The following are some issues:

- **Inconsistent pattern for messaging and orchestration**: The messages that fail during the processing of the messaging engine (during the execution of a pipeline for example) get suspended or, if **Failed Messages Routing** is enabled in the corresponding port, routed to failed messages subscribers. In our orchestrations we don't have the same feature. We could create our own exception handling blocks to promote the same context properties **Failed Messages Routing** does, so the behavior was somehow similar, but we would still need to create those exception handling libraries so those were re-usable across orchestrations. Now we don't need to worry about that as the ESB Toolkit provides that API and standardized and proven patterns to follow.

- Limited alerting features: The best we could get when something goes wrong would be an event being logged in the Windows Event Viewer or some suspended instances showing up in the BizTalk Administration Console, but we would need to rely on further customization to get the correct people notified. We could do this either with custom code or some other monitoring products such as **System Center Operations Manager** (SCOM), but yet again the Toolkit comes to the rescue with some prebuilt features for this.

- Access to the error information: Some individuals within the organization might need to review and even report on the errors on our solution, but that would require granting them access to our production environment or relying on other solutions to provide the appropriate information.

- Issues resolution: The process of saving failed messages, manually fixing them, and resubmitting them is not always very neat, so a bit of extra help in here is more than welcome as well.

In the following figure we can see, highlighted in dashed square boxes, that the different areas of the ESB Toolkit architecture bring some cool news features around exception handing to tackle the issues mentioned earlier:

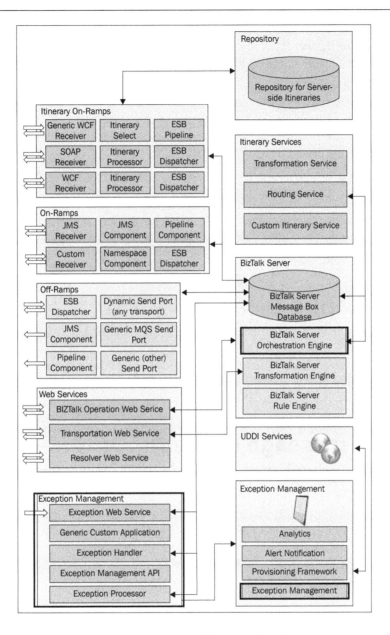

Those main items will be described in detail later in this chapter:

- The Exception Handling API: The ESB Toolkit provides an API that establishes defined patterns to deal with errors that might happen within the ESB and generate a fault message for them, either on the messaging or the orchestration runtime.

- The Exception Management Pipeline Components: These pipeline components preprocess any fault message published into the ESB, that later will be published into the ESB Management portal through the ESB Exception database.

- The ESB Management Portal: One of the main features of the portal is to provide reporting features over the errors that might happen in our portal, as well as creating alerts to be triggered when certain errors happen and even resubmitting failed messages.

- The Exception Web Service: Allows external systems to publish their own exceptions into the ESB.

By using all these features, we can envision and implement our error handling model in our ESB solution, even being able to establish an organization-wide standardized model to handle and report business errors.

The Exception Handling API

As we mentioned before, in order to provide a more convenient approach to handle our exceptions in BizTalk, we would need to write some custom code and define the patterns our development team should follow to use them. Over time this has been done by many teams around the world, but now there's no need to reinvent the wheel as this is provided by the ESB Toolkit.

The fault message concept

The whole exception handling feature in the ESB Toolkit is built around the fault message concept.

A fault message is a special type of message that contains all the information about the failure that happened while processing at some point in our ESB. It's the canonical representation of a failure in the ESB, and contains all the relevant information about the fault and its schema is `Microsoft.Practices.ESB.ExceptionHandling.Schemas.Reporting.FaultMessage`.

Failed messages can come from three different sources, and so they need to be normalized so any downstream components know how to handle them and the data they contain.

Fault messages originated by the messaging runtime

These are the already known failed messages generated by the **Failed Messages Routing** feature, which have the following properties added to their context:

- `FailureCode`
- `FailureCategory`
- `Description`
- `MessageType`
- `ReceivePortName`
- `InboundTransportLocation`
- `SendPortName`
- `OutboundTransportLocation`
- `ErrorType`
- `RoutingFailureReportID`

Fault messages explicitly instantiated in code

These are instantiated using the `Microsoft.Practices.ESB.ExceptionHandling.ExceptionMgmt.CreateFaultMessage` method of the API within an exception handling block in an orchestration. This generates a new BizTalk message whose schema is `Microsoft.Practices.ESB.ExceptionHandling.Schemas.Faults.FaultMessage`. The message has the following parts:

- Automatic fault properties: This schema defines the following properties for the fault message that are auto populated when the message is created:
  - `Application`: The name of the application where the fault happened
  - `DateTime`: The UTC moment in time when the fault happened
  - `Description`: The description of the exception that caused the fault
  - `ErrorType`: The type of fault
  - `MachineName`: The name of the server where the fault actually happened
  - `Scope`: The `Scope` shape that contains the current exception handler
  - `ServiceName`: The service where the message failed (orchestration name)
  - `ServiceInstanceID`: The GUID of the service instance within BizTalk where the fault happened

- Explicit fault properties: Some more properties that have to be added explicitly in the code after the message is created. The values set in those will depend on our solution error definitions:

  ○ `FaultCategory`: The category of the fault

  ○ `FaultCode`: The code that identifies the specific type of fault

  ○ `FaultSeverity`: The severity of the fault (defined by the `Microsoft. Practices.ESB.ExceptionHandling.FaultSeverity` enumeration)

  ○ `FaultDescription`: The description we want to give to the actual fault, that might be different from the exception message

 Note that leaving any of the fault properties with a null value will cause the serialization of the message to fail.

- The exception: The exception that caused the fault itself gets automatically serialized into the fault message.

- Attached messages: Using the `Microsoft.Practices.ESB. ExceptionHandling.ExceptionMgmt.AddMessage` method we can add the message or messages that were being processed when the exception happened. Those are added as additional parts to the fault message.

In the following diagram, we can see the exception handling block of the `EAIProcess.odx` sample orchestration included in the Exception Handling sample solution from the ESB Toolkit. On that block, the standard pattern to handle exceptions is followed and likewise can be replicated in your own orchestrations:

1. Construct the fault message:

   ○ Use the `CreateFaultMessage` to instantiate the message. The destination message variable has to be of a multipart message type whose body part type is `Microsoft.Practices.ESB. ExceptionHandling.Schemas.Faults.FaultMessage`.

   ○ Populate the `FaultCategory`, `FaultCode`, `FaultSeverity`, and `FaultDescription` properties.

   ○ Attach any messages that are relevant to the processing where the fault happened.

2. Send the fault message to the message box through a direct bound send port, so any downstream subscribers process it. That port has to send messages of the multipart message type mentioned earlier.

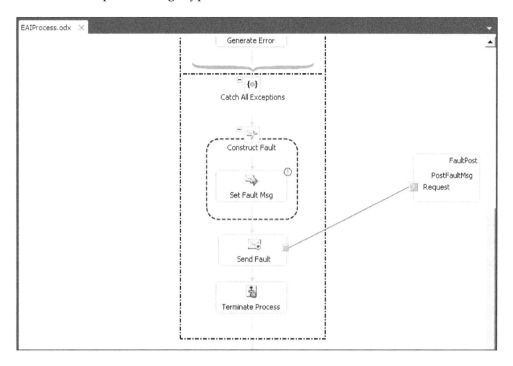

Fault messages published by other systems through the ESB Exceptions Service

These faults are received right away from external applications that might call the ESB Exceptions Service. This service just exposes the `Microsoft.Practices.ESB. ExceptionHandling.Schemas.Reporting.FaultMessage` canonical schema, so the callers provide all the relevant information about the fault. We will explain more about the fault canonical schema in the next section, and about the ESB Exceptions Service by the end of the chapter.

The fault canonical schema

As we mentioned earlier, this is the schema any fault message is converted to in order to homogenize the structure of the faults despite of where they were generated. The information is just pulled from the incoming fault message and populated into the following fragments of the message:

- Header: This fragment contains the basic properties of the fault (some of those already described before in the chapter):
  - ° `Application`
  - ° `Description`
  - ° `ErrorType`
  - ° `FailureCategory`
  - ° `FaultCode`
  - ° `FaultDescription`
  - ° `FaultSeverity`
  - ° `Scope`
  - ° `ServiceInstanceID`
  - ° `ServiceName`
  - ° `MachineName`
  - ° `DateTime`
  - ° `ControlBit`
  - ° `MessageID`
  - ° `ActivityIdentity`
  - ° `NACK`: Set to `true` if the fault was caused by a `NACK`
  - ° `FaultGenerator`: The type of service where the fault happened (for example, Messaging or Orchestration)
- Exception Object: Is the serialized representation of the exception that caused the fault.
- Messages: Contains any messages attached to the fault. This section includes the following properties of each message:
  - ° `ContentType`
  - ° `MessageName`
  - ° `RoutingURL`
  - ° `MessageContext`

- ° MessageID
- ° InterchangeID
- ° MessageType
- ° MessageData

We will see later in this chapter how this transformation into the fault canonical form is undertaken by the Exception Encoder pipeline component.

Exception Handling API main methods

The API exposes through the ESB.ExceptionHandling assembly the methods required to deal with fault messages. Those methods are:

- CreateFaultMessage: Creates an ESB fault message as an XLANGMessage instance with all the properties and data described in the previous section. It's meant to be used within an orchestration exception handling block.

> Note that the usage of the CreateFaultMessage method *outside of an exception handling block is not supported* and will make your orchestration get into an endless loop and making the CPU go to 100 percent on the corresponding host instance process. If you really need to do it, the best option to do so without having to actually get into modifying the ESB Toolkit code is to throw your own exception when needed and keep using the method within an Exception Handling block.
>
> We shouldn't consider approaches that imply disassembling and modifying the ESB Toolkit binaries, as that *would break the software license*.

- AddMessage: Takes as parameters two XLANGMessage instances; the first is a newly-created ESB fault message, and the second is any existing message instance in the orchestration. The method persists the existing message instance and its message context properties into the fault message and makes it available for retrieval using the GetMessage method. It's meant to be used within an orchestration exception handling block.

- SetException: Takes as parameters an ESB fault message as an XLANGMessage instance and Exception as an Object instance. The method persists the exception into the existing fault message and makes it available for retrieval using the GetException method. It's meant to be used within an orchestration exception handling block.

- GetMessage: Takes as parameters an ESB fault message as an XLANGMessage instance and the (String) name of the message previously added to the fault message (in the exception handler of the originating orchestration shape). Returns an XLANGMessage instance that matches the message name and that contains all the original context properties, including any custom promoted properties.

- GetMessages: Takes as the single parameter an ESB fault message as an XLANGMessage instance. Returns a MessageCollection instance populated with all the XLANGMessage instances previously added to the fault message (in the exception handler of the originating orchestration shape). Each XLANGMessage instance contains all the original context properties, including any custom promoted properties.

- GetException: Takes as the single parameter a fault message as an XLANGMessage instance. Returns the System.Exception object previously added to the fault message (in the exception handler of the originating orchestration shape).

Consuming fault messages

Earlier in the chapter we saw how to produce a fault message by means of the API. The counterpart of that process would be consuming the fault message in an orchestration or a port that subscribes to that fault message.

The ESB Toolkit includes a send port named ALL.Exceptions that processes fault messages produced in any of the three ways mentioned before (messaging failure, orchestration exception handling or ESB Exceptions Service). The filter of that send port is quite simple, but we could create our own fault message subscribers, with more granular filters if required.

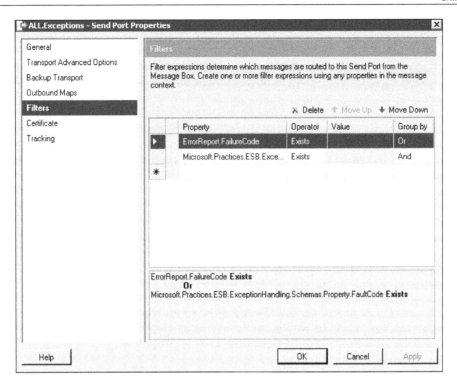

The ESB Fault Processor pipeline

The ESB Toolkit includes a re-usable pipeline component, named **ESB Exception Encoder**, that can be used in our solution to process fault messages received by a send port and normalize them into the fault canonical form we described earlier in the chapter.

This pipeline component is used by the ESB Fault Processor pipeline, which is also included in the ESB Toolkit. This send pipeline also uses the ESB Dispatcher and ESB BAM Tracker pipeline components to prepare the fault messages to be published into the ESBExceptionDb database. Finally, this pipeline is used by the ALL.Exceptions send port to actually send those faults into that database. We will describe now the role played by each of the pipeline components used in the ESB Fault Processor pipeline.

ESB Exception Encoder component

This pipeline component has the duty of turning fault messages generated in three different ways (messaging failure, orchestration exception handling, or ESB Exceptions Service) into the fault canonical form, homogenizing their information and structure.

For fault messages generated in an orchestration or submitted by means of the ESB Exceptions Service, the component enriches and serializes all fault message properties, XLANG messages, context properties, and `System.Exception` information into an XML message.

For fault messages coming from the Failed Message Routing executed in a messaging interaction, the component enriches the data by adding the application name and other ambient properties. It also applies the schema namespace to the outbound XML message content.

This pipeline component has three properties that can be configured on it:

- `FaultDocumentNamespace`. Defined the namespace of the fault message schema. By default it is `http://schemas.microsoft.biztalk.practices.esb.com/exceptionhandling` but can be changed if we create our own custom outbound namespace for the persisted messages.

- `ProcessingInstruction`: The ESB Toolkit includes a sample `InfoPath` form where the fault messages can be viewed. In order to be displayed in the `InfoPath` form, the fault messages XML has to include an `InfoPath` processing instruction. The default processing instruction to be used with this sample form is the one shown as follows, but we can use our own to use our own `InfoPath` forms:

```
<?mso-infoPathSolution solutionVersion="1.0.0.346"
productVersion="11.0.6565"
PIVersion="1.0.0.0"
href=file:///\\localhost\publish\Microsoft.Practices.ESB.
ExceptionHandling.InfoPath.Reporting.xsn
name="urn:schemas-microsoft-com:office:infopath:
Microsoft-Practices-ESB-ExceptionHandling-InfoPath-Reporting:
http---schemas-microsoft-biztalk-practices-esb-com-
exceptionhandling"
language="en-us" ?><?mso-application progid="InfoPath.Document"?>
```

- `EscapeCDATA`: Any CDATA sections in the messages attached to the fault are escaped if this property is set to `true`. This will allow `InfoPath` to display them correctly.

This pipeline component can be included in our own pipelines, by adding it to the Encode stage of them.

ESB BAM Tracker component

As we described in *Chapter 2, Itinerary Services*, this component can be used to capture fault messages information into our BAM database. The fields that are published as part of the corresponding activity record are Application, ErrorType, DateTime, FailureCategory, Description, FaultCode, FaultDescription, FaultGenerator, FaultSeverity, MachineName, Scope, ServiceInstanceID, ServiceName, and MessageID. The MessageID field becomes the activity ID.

Through the component's properties, we can enable/disable the component (by means of the Enabled property) or define a custom namespace for the fault messages (defined on the FaultDocumentNamespace property), so the component can extract the data from our custom schemas.

ESB Dispatcher

The ALL.Exceptions port delivers the fault messages to the ESBExceptionDb database through the SQL adapter. The SQL adapter needs to receive a message in the form of an updategram, so it knows how to make the corresponding operations in SQL. The updategram structure used to insert faults information into the ESBExceptionsDb is defined by the ExceptionSql.xsd schema.

 Note that the ALL.Exceptions port uses the legacy SQL Adapter, not the WCF-SQL Adapter.

In consequence, our canonical form faults need to be transformed into that updategram. This is achieved by using the ESB Dispatcher component, with its MapName property set to the corresponding map included in the ESB Toolkit:

```
Microsoft.Practices.ESB.ExceptionHandling.Maps.FaultMessage_to_
ExceptionSql,
Microsoft.Practices.ESB.ExceptionHandling.Maps,
Version=1.0.0.0,
Culture=neutral,
PublicKeyToken=c2c8b2b87f54180a
```

Consuming a fault in an orchestration

We can implement our own orchestrations subscribing to fault messages to make any processing that might be required (for example, it could orchestrate the interaction with our production issues case management system and our TFS bugs repository).

Using the Exception Handling API, we can access the messages that were being processed as well as the exception that originally caused the fault. With that information and the rest of the fault message properties, our exception handler can implement the process defined by the solution design of our operation's model.

In the following image, we can see a similar approach, where the process is as follows:

1. We receive the fault message.
2. We retrieve the messages attached to the fault.
3. We construct a message for our production issues case management system and send it through.
4. We wait to receive the result of the evaluation of the case.
   - If the case is evaluated within our defined SLA (Service Level Agreement, that could be set to 8 hours, and needless to say it shouldn't be hardcoded in a constant as a good coding practice), we check if the evaluation stated that the fault was caused by a bug in the solution.
   - If we have a bug, we create the corresponding TFS web services request and send it through to create the bug in TFS.
   - If it was not a bug, but caused by some invalid data in the message, the original message is sent to be repaired by the operations team.
   - If the SLA expires, the case is escalated by notifying it to the escalation manager.

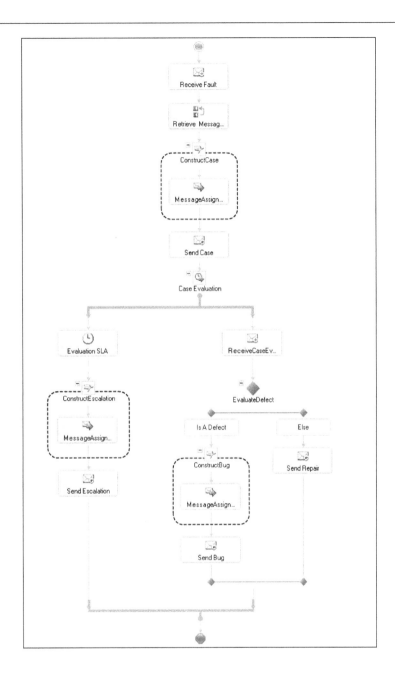

The ESB Management Portal

The ESB Management Portal consumes data from the `ESBExceptionDb` database where the faults information is published. This data feeds several features in the portal.

 The ESB Management Portal is one of the samples provided with the toolkit and might not fit all organizations' needs, so it's open for any customizations required.

Fault reports

This module within the portal shows different reports about the faults that happened in our ESB. All the reports are accessible through the **Reports** link on the portal navigation bar, and can be filtered by application and by time range. The following reports listed are shown in the picture from left to right and from top to bottom:

- **Fault Count By Application**: This report displays an aggregate view of all the faults generated for a specified set of applications over a specified time. This report is also shown in the portal's home page.

- **Fault Count By Error Type**: This report displays an aggregate view of all faults by specified error type generated for a specified set of applications over a specified time. This report is also shown in the portal's home page.

- **Fault Count Over Time**: This report displays a count of faults over a specified period for a specified set of applications. You can select an application to display a trend chart showing the number of faults over time for specific services within the application. This report is also shown in the portal's home page.

- **Alert Count By Application**: This report displays an aggregate view of all the alerts generated for a specified set of applications over a specified time.

- **Resubmissions Over Time**: This report displays a count of failed message resubmissions over a specified period for a specified set of applications.

- **Alert Subscriptions Over Time**: This report displays a count of alert subscriptions over a specified period for a specified set of applications.

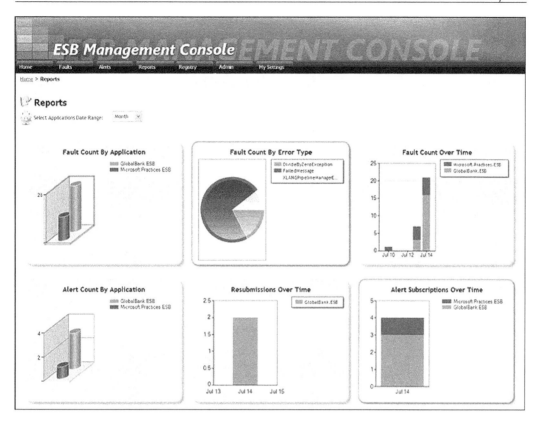

Faults list

The faults list page shows the list of the faults that happened in our ESB. We can filter and sort the results to find the items that we are interested in, and we can even export the list to Excel.

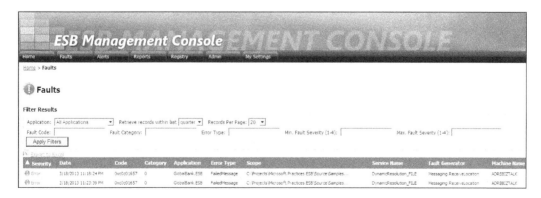

By clicking on any of the line items, we access to the **Fault Viewer**, where we can inspect the data of the fault, and at the bottom we have links to the messages that were attached to the fault.

If we click on any of the attached messages links in the **Fault Viewer**, we access to the **Message Viewer**. On this page we can:

- Inspect the information of the message, including its contents and context properties

- Download the message

- Edit the message

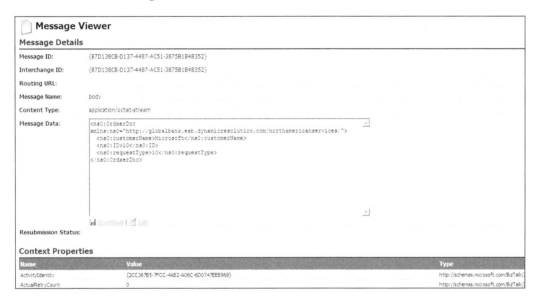

By clicking on the **Edit** link, we are able to edit the contents of the message (for example, to correct some invalid data). Once we finish repairing our message, we can resubmit it directly to the ESB through two receive locations that are created when the ESB Toolkit is installed (or any custom receive locations we might create for resubmission).

We need to keep in mind that this feature could expose a possible security threat if access to the portal is not restricted to the appropriate user groups that should be undertaking these operations.

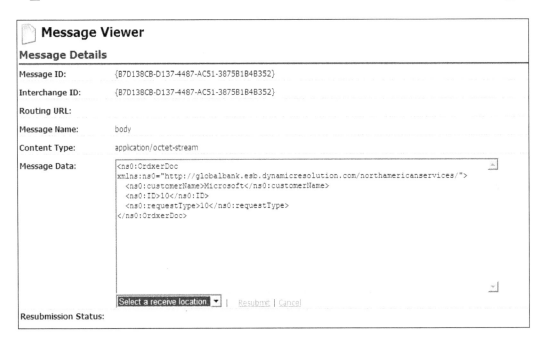

A simplified view of this list is also shown in the portal's home page.

Alerts

The ESB Toolkit has a feature to notify us when certain faults happen if we create an alert for them. On this page, we can view a list of the alerts that we created in the past or create new ones.

The alerts triggering criteria can be composed by logical conditions based on the fault fields.

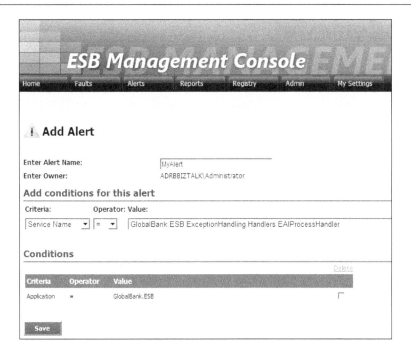

Once an alert is created, we can add subscribers to it. They will be notified, once the alert is triggered, on the specified e-mail address according to the schedule set on the subscription.

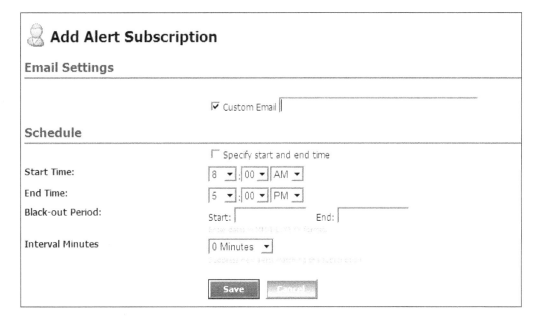

Exceptions web service

In some organizations, the errors that happen in some systems might be relevant to other systems (for example, our production support case management system in the Exception Handler sample that we showed earlier in the chapter). Thanks to the ESB Exceptions service, we can standardize our operations processes in a company-wide fashion by having a unified process to notify and react to issues that happen in our systems.

External systems can use this web service to submit their own errors to the ESB. They just need to invoke the web service providing the relevant information of the fault that happened in the system, and so the fault message will be published into the ESB, allowing any subscribers to receive it and process it as required.

The service is deployed in two flavors when the ESB Toolkit is installed, providing both SOAP and WCF endpoints. The following figure shows the two types of services:

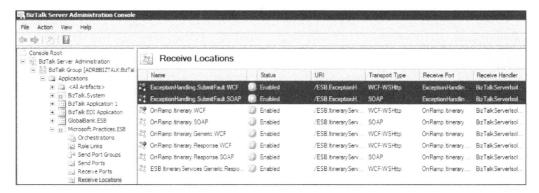

Summary

In this chapter, we learned how the ESB Toolkit helps us to design and implement a consistent error handling model within our ESB.

In the next chapter, we will go through the additional web services provided by the ESB Toolkit that support some other use cases for our ESB.

4
Understanding the ESB
Web Services

One of the main goals of an ESB is to facilitate access to the services and capabilities exposed by IT solutions across an organization. In order to facilitate access to those services, the ESB Toolkit provides a set of services that enable consumers to participate in ESB message exchanges through a standardized API. At the same time, some of the ESB Toolkit core features are exposed as services.

In this chapter we will:

- Explore the different services exposed by the ESB Toolkit
- Analyze the scenarios where those services can be useful to external systems

The itinerary on-ramp services

The **itinerary** web services, also known as **on-ramps**, are the ones that allow clients trigger ESB exchanges and processes by delivering messages to the ESB for their processing.

The main inputs to trigger the message processing by an itinerary in the ESB are:

- The payload: It's the actual message that is meant to be processed. When using the out of the box Itinerary web services, this payload must be an XML document, but we could create our own itinerary service to receive non-XML payloads for processing through itineraries. These could be meant to process flat files or other kinds of files.

- The itinerary: We need to tell the service which itinerary the payload should go through. We can do it explicitly by attaching the actual itinerary XML representation, or by providing the information required to resolve the itinerary to be used. The ESB Toolkit provides two sets of services (in WCF and ASMX flavors) that support these two ways to specify the itinerary.

Itinerary.SOAP and Itinerary.Response.SOAP

These two services allow clients to submit a payload to be processed by an itinerary that is explicitly defined by the client. They are respectively meant to execute one-way and request-response itineraries. The itinerary XML definition is attached to the web service request as a SOAP header.

Once we add the service reference to those web services in our code, the class that defines that SOAP header is represented by the `Itinerary` class, as shown in the following screenshot:

```
Reference.cs  ×

ESB.Itinerary.Test.asmxItineraryOneWay.Itinerary          ▼   resolverGroupsField

    /// <remarks/>
    [System.CodeDom.Compiler.GeneratedCodeAttribute("System.Xml", "4.0.30319.18034")]
    [System.SerializableAttribute()]
    [System.Diagnostics.DebuggerStepThroughAttribute()]
    [System.ComponentModel.DesignerCategoryAttribute("code")]
    [System.Xml.Serialization.XmlTypeAttribute(AnonymousType=true, Namespace="http://schemas.microsoft.biztalk.pra
    [System.Xml.Serialization.XmlRootAttribute(Namespace="http://schemas.microsoft.biztalk.practices.esb.com/itine
    public partial class Itinerary : System.Web.Services.Protocols.SoapHeader {

        private ItineraryBizTalkSegment bizTalkSegmentField;

        private ItineraryServiceInstance serviceInstanceField;

        private ItineraryServices[] servicesField;

        private ArrayOfItineraryResolversResolvers[] resolverGroupsField;

        private ArrayOfItineraryPropertyProperty[] propertyBagField;

        private string uuidField;

        private string beginTimeField;

        private string completeTimeField;

        private string stateField;

        private bool isRequestResponseField;

        private bool isRequestResponseFieldSpecified;

100 %  ▼
```

To populate the `Itinerary` class instance that will be attached as a SOAP header, we can either instantiate the `Itinerary` class and fill out by code all it properties (itinerary services that compose the itinerary, resolvers to be used by the itinerary, and so on) or just deserialize the itinerary specification from an XML file. This last approach is a much easier and maintainable one.

So given the XML definition as shown in the following XML file:

```xml
<?xml version="1.0" encoding="utf-8" ?>
<Itinerary xmlns:xsi="http://www.w3.org/2001/XMLSchema-instance"
  xmlns:xsd="http://www.w3.org/2001/XMLSchema" uuid="" beginTime="" completeTime="" state="Pending"
  isRequestResponse="false" xmlns="http://schemas.microsoft.biztalk.practices.esb.com/itinerary">
  <ServiceInstance uuid="" name="Microsoft.Practices.ESB.Services.Transform" type="Messaging"
    state="Pending" position="0" isRequestResponse="false" xmlns="" />
  <Services xmlns="">
    <Service uuid="" beginTime="" completeTime="" name="Microsoft.Practices.ESB.Services.Transform"
      type="Messaging" state="Pending" isRequestResponse="false" position="0" serviceInstanceId="" />
  </Services>
  <Services xmlns="">
    <Service uuid="" beginTime="" completeTime="" name="Microsoft.Practices.ESB.Services.Routing"
      type="Messaging" state="Pending" isRequestResponse="false" position="1" serviceInstanceId="" />
  </Services>
  <Services xmlns="">
    <Service uuid="" beginTime="" completeTime="" name="DynamicResolutionSolicitResp"
      type="Messaging" state="Pending" isRequestResponse="true" position="2" serviceInstanceId="" />
  </Services>
  <ResolverGroups xmlns="">
    <Resolvers serviceId="Microsoft.Practices.ESB.Services.Routing1"><![CDATA
      [BRE:\\policy=GetCanadaEndPoint;version=;useMsg=;]]></Resolvers>
    <Resolvers serviceId="Microsoft.Practices.ESB.Services.Transform0"><![CDATA
      [BRE:\\policy=CanadaSubmitOrderMaps;version=;useMsg=;]]></Resolvers>
    <Resolvers serviceId="DynamicResolutionSolicitResp2" />
  </ResolverGroups>
</Itinerary>
```

We just need to deserialize its contents into the corresponding `Itinerary` class instance, and use it right away in the web service proxy instance that we will use to call the service, as shown in the following example:

```
XmlDocument payload = new XmlDocument();
payload.Load("myPayload.xml");

asmxItineraryTwoWay.Process svc = new asmxItineraryTwoWay.Process();
svc.Credentials = System.Net.CredentialCache.DefaultCredentials;

XmlDocument itdoc = new XmlDocument();
itdoc.Load("myItineraryXML.XML");
string ItineraryStr = itdoc.DocumentElement.OuterXml;


StringReader reader = new StringReader(ItineraryStr);
```

```
XmlSerializer ser = new XmlSerializer(typeof(asmxItineraryTwoWay.
Itinerary),
   http://schemas.microsoft.biztalk.practices.esb.com/itinerary");
asmxItineraryTwoWay.Itinerary itnryTwoWay = (asmxItineraryTwoWay.
Itinerary)ser.Deserialize(reader);

svc.ItineraryValue = itnryTwoWay;
XmlNode node = (XmlNode)payload;

svc.SubmitRequestResponse(ref node);
```

As the web service request reaches the On-Ramp receive location for the service, the `ItineraryReceiveXml` pipeline configured in that receive location processes the message received. Within that pipeline, the ESB Itinerary Pipeline component is the one in charge of extracting the itinerary definition received as a SOAP header, and promoting its information into the message context, so the message can follow the usual itinerary processing logic.

Itinerary.WCF and Itinerary.Response.WCF

These services are similar to the previous ones, but these have a different pipeline configured on their receive location, the `ItinerarySelectReceiveXml` pipeline. This pipeline has the ESB Itinerary Select pipeline component, that allows the client just to specify the name (and optionally the version) of the itinerary, and the component automatically retrieves the itinerary definition from the `Itineraries` repository. The following example shows how we could consume these services in our client application:

```
using (ItineraryTwoWayService.ProcessRequestResponseClient client =
new ItineraryTwoWayService.ProcessRequestResponseClient("WSHttpBindi
ng_ITwoWayAsync"))
{
  XmlDocument payload = new XmlDocument();
  payload.Load("myPayload.xml");
  object response = payload.OuterXml;


  itinDesc = new ItineraryTwoWayService.ItineraryDescription();
  itinDesc.Name = genericItineraryName;
  itinDesc.Version = genericItineraryVersion;
  itinDesc.Guid = Guid.NewGuid().ToString();
  txtTrackingID.Text = itinDesc.Guid;

  client.SubmitRequestResponse(itinDesc, ref response);
}
```

ItineraryServices.Generic.WCF and ItineraryServices.Generic.Response.WCF

The pipeline configured on these two uses the ESB Itinerary Selector pipeline components, but uses it in a slightly different way.

They don't receive an itinerary description as a header that defines the name of the itinerary, but they rely on the resolver connection string configured on the ESB Itinerary Selector pipeline component to dynamically resolve the itinerary.

We could use a BRI connection string in the `ResolverConnectionString` of the pipeline component. The connection string could look like the following:

```
BRI:\\policy=policyName;version=1.0;useMsg=true
```

When the call arrives at the service, the pipeline component will execute the dynamic resolution by means of the BRE policy specified on it, using the contents of the message as an input for the policy. The policy will resolve the itinerary name and version according to our business rule, and retrieve the actual itinerary from the `Itineraries` repository. Finally, the itinerary information is promoted to the message context.

The Resolver web service

The ESB Toolkit provides us with a powerful and dynamic resolution framework that helps us to discover how our ESB interactions should behave. For example, deciding which endpoint should be reached by some message or which transformation should be applied.

This capability can be very useful to be re-used by any external systems connected to the ESB, and so this Resolver web service exposes it to any consumer. Like the Itinerary services, this service is exposed in both ASMX and WCF flavors.

The service has two operations:

- `Resolve`: This operation executes the resolution using as an input the connection string exclusively, and so that's the only parameter it takes as an input. The service executes the corresponding resolver and returns the resolution result as a list of name-value pairs.

- `ResolveMessage`: This operation, apart from the resolution connection string, receives an XML message as a string. That message is used as an input for the resolution process (for example, a BRE resolver that checks certain values inside the input message) and the same way the result of the resolution is returned as a list of name-value pairs.

The Transformation web service

This service exposes the ESB feature of messages transformation. It does so without needing to persist the actual message into the message box to do it.

It has one single operation named Transform that takes as an input the XML message to be transformed and the fully qualified name of the map deployed in BizTalk. It returns the XML representation of the transformed message.

Systems consuming this service shouldn't necessarily need to know the format in which the maps' names are qualified in BizTalk, so it could be useful to use the Resolver service to resolve the name of the map, and then use the output of that resolution as an input for the fully qualified name of the map on the Transform call.

This service is also available in both ASMX and WCF flavors.

The Exception Handling web service

This service was already introduced in the *Chapter 3, ESB Exception Handling*, dedicated to the exception management in the ESB Toolkit.

In order to submit a fault into the ESB so it's handled by the standard ESB faults processing logic we might have in place in our ESB, we just need to instantiate the `FaultMessage` class defined in the service contract, fill its properties, and use it as an input for the `SubmitFault` operation of the service.

The properties on that fault message are the same as the ones we already described in the *Chapter 3, ESB Exception Handling*:

```
Ex.ExceptionHandling handleException = new ExceptionHandlingService.
SubmitFault.ExceptionHandling();
                handleException.Credentials = System.Net.
CredentialCache.DefaultCredentials;


                Ex.FaultMessage faultMsg = new Ex.FaultMessage();
                faultMsg.Header = new Ex.FaultMessageHeader();
                faultMsg.Header.Application = "Exception Handling
Service Test";
                faultMsg.Header.Description = "Fault Message Header";
                faultMsg.Header.ErrorType = "Error Type";
                faultMsg.Header.FaultSeverity = 1;
                faultMsg.Header.FaultCode = "Fault Code";
                faultMsg.Header.FailureCategory = "Failure Category";
                faultMsg.Header.FaultDescription = "Fault
Description;";
```

```
                faultMsg.Header.FaultGenerator = "Fault Generator";
                faultMsg.Header.Scope = "Fault Message Scope";
                faultMsg.Header.ServiceInstanceID = System.Guid.
NewGuid().ToString();
                faultMsg.Header.ServiceName = "Exception Service";
                faultMsg.Header.MachineName = System.Environment.
MachineName;
                faultMsg.Header.DateTime = System.DateTime.Now.
ToString();
                faultMsg.Header.ControlBit = "1";
                faultMsg.Header.MessageID = System.Guid.NewGuid().
ToString();
                faultMsg.Header.ActivityIdentity = "Activity Identity
";
                faultMsg.Header.NACK = false;


                Ex.ExceptionHandling exceptionHandler = new
Ex.ExceptionHandling();
                faultMsg.ExceptionObject = new Ex.FaultMessageExcepti
onObject();
                faultMsg.ExceptionObject.Message = "Exception Messge";
                faultMsg.ExceptionObject.Source = "Exception Source";
                faultMsg.ExceptionObject.Type = "Exception Type";
                faultMsg.ExceptionObject.TargetSite = "Exception
Target";
                faultMsg.ExceptionObject.StackTrace = "Exception Stack
Trace";
                faultMsg.ExceptionObject.InnerExceptionMessage =
"Inner Exception Message";

                List<Ex.
ArrayOfFaultMessageMessageContextPropertyContextProperty>
contexts = new List<Ex.
ArrayOfFaultMessageMessageContextPropertyContextProperty>()
                {
                    new Ex.ArrayOfFaultMessageMessageContextPropertyCo
ntextProperty{Name = "Context Name1", Type = "Context Type1", Value =
"Context Value1"},
                    new Ex.ArrayOfFaultMessageMessageContextPropertyCo
ntextProperty{Name = "Context Name2", Type = "Context Type2", Value =
"Context Value2"}
                };
```

```
              Ex.ArrayOfFaultMessageMessageMessageMessageData
messagedata = new Ex.ArrayOfFaultMessageMessageMessageMessageData();
              XmlDocument xmldoc = new XmlDocument();
              // XmlDocumentFragment fragIn = xmldoc.
CreateDocumentFragment();
              xmldoc.LoadXml("<Order><customerName>Microsoft</
customerName><ID>10</ID><requestType>10</requestType></Order>");
              XmlNode[] anyField = new System.Xml.XmlNode[1];
              anyField[0] = (XmlNode)xmldoc;
              messagedata.Any = anyField;



              List<Ex.ArrayOfFaultMessageMessageMessage> messages =
new List<Ex.ArrayOfFaultMessageMessageMessage>()
              {
                  new Ex.ArrayOfFaultMessageMessageMessage{Con
tentType = "text/xml",InterchangeID = "InterchangeID1",MessageID
= "MessageID1",MessageName = "MessageName1",MessageType =
"MessageType1",MessageContext = contexts.ToArray(),MessageData =
messagedata},
                  new Ex.ArrayOfFaultMessageMessageMessage{Con
tentType = "text/xml",InterchangeID = "InterchangeID2",MessageID
= "MessageID2",MessageName = "MessageName2",MessageType =
"MessageType2",MessageContext = contexts.ToArray(),MessageData =
messagedata}
              };


              faultMsg.Messages = messages.ToArray();
              handleException.SubmitFault(faultMsg);
```

This service is also available in both ASMX and WCF flavors.

The BizTalk Operations web service

The BizTalk Operations web service exposes to external systems information about our ESB environment, the artifacts deployed on it, and the messages flowing through our ESB.

This could be useful to provide information to our own operations and management systems.

It exposes the following operations:

- `Applications`: This method is without parameters. It returns the name and description of all the installed BizTalk applications as a collection of `BTApplication` objects.

- `ApplicationStatus`: This method has one parameter, the application name. It returns information about the specified BizTalk application as a `BTSysStatus` instance. This includes orchestrations, send ports, receive locations, and host details.

- `GetLiveMessageBody`: This method takes two parameters, message ID and instance ID. It returns the body of that message from the live environment as a `BTMsgBody` instance.

- `GetMessageInstances`: This method takes one parameter, the message type It returns all matching messages as a collection of `BTMsgInstance` objects.

- `GetOrchestrationInstances`: This method takes one parameter, the name of an orchestration. It returns a collection of `BTOrchestrationInstance` object that contain details of the orchestration input.

- `GetTrackedMessageBody`: This method takes one parameter, a message GUID. It returns the body of that message as a `BTMsgBody` instance after BizTalk processes it.

- `Hosts`: This method takes a single parameter, the name of a host. It returns information about the specified host instance as in a collection of `BTHost` instances. If you input an empty string, it will return information about all host instances.

- `MessageFlowTree`: This method takes as a single parameter, an instance ID. It returns details of the message flow for that message as a `RouteTreeNode` instance.

- `Orchestrations`: This method takes as a single parameter, orchestration name. It returns all the information for that orchestration as a `BTSysStatus` instance. If you input an empty string, it will return information about all orchestrations.

- `ReceiveLocations`: This method takes as a single parameter, receive location name. It returns all the information for matching locations as a `BTSysStatus` instance. If you imput an empty string, it will return information about all locations.

- `ReceiveLocationsByDescription`: This method takes as a single parameter, the description of a receive location. It returns all the information for matching locations as a `BTSysStatus` instance. If you imput an empty string, it will return information about all locations.

- `SendPorts`: This method takes as a single parameter, send port name. It returns all the information for matching ports as a `BTSysStatus` instance. If you imput an empty string, it will return information about all ports.

- `SendPortsByDescription`: This method takes as a parameter the description of a send port, and it returns all the information for matching ports as a `BTSysStatus` instance. Use an empty string, it will return information about all ports.

- `StatusChanged`: This method takes as a single parameter, a timestamp. It returns details of BizTalk objects (such as ports, hosts, and orchestrations) modified since the specified timestamp as a `BTSysStatus` instance.

- `SystemStatus`: This method is without parameters. It returns full details of the BizTalk system status as a `BTSysStatus` instance.

- `UpdateReceiveLocationDescription`: This method does an update of the description of a specified receive location. It uses parameter values that contain the application name, the receive port name, the receive location name, and the receive location description. It returns a String value that indicates the result of the operation. Note that the test client application reads this information from its `App.config` file.

- `UpdateSendPortDescription`: This method updates the description of a specified send port using parameter values that contain the send port name and the send port description. It returns a String that indicates the result of the operation. Note that the test client application reads this information from its `App.config` file.

Summary

In this chapter, we went through the different web services exposed by the ESB Toolkit, learned what their capabilities are, and saw how we can consume them.

In the next chapter, we will further describe the features of the ESB Management Portal that were briefly introduced in the previous chapters.

5
The ESB Management Portal

We already discussed some of the features provided by the ESB Management Portal in *Chapter 3*, *ESB Exception Handling*, where we explored the exception handling features of the ESB Toolkit. Apart from those, the ESB portal provides some other main capabilities around publishing our services endpoints into **UDDI**, as well as configuring different parameters that drive the behavior of the portal.

For those not familiar with UDDI, it is an abbreviation for **Universal Description Discovery and Integration**. More information can be found on Wikipedia at http://en.wikipedia.org/wiki/Universal_Description_Discovery_and_Integration.

In this chapter we will:

- Learn how to publish endpoints into UDDI from the ESB Management Portal
- Learn the ESB Portal Audit Log
- Explore the different parameterizations that we can do on the portal

Registering services in UDDI

Thanks to the ESB Toolkit, we can easily populate our organization's services registry in UDDI with the services that interact with the ESB, either because the ESB exposes them or because they can be consumed through it.

Before we can register service in UDDI we must first configure the registry settings.

Registry settings

The registry settings change how the UDDI registration functionality mentioned in preceding section behaves.

- **UDDI Server**: This sets URL of the UDDI server.

- **Auto Publish**: When enabled, any registry request will be automatically published. If it's disabled, the requests will require administrative approval.

- **Anonymous**: This setting indicates whether to use anonymous access to connect to the UDDI server or to use the UDDI Publisher Service account.

- **Notification Enabled**: This enables or disables the delivery of notifications when any registry activity occurs on the portal.

- **SMTP Server**: This is the address of the SMTP server that will send notification e-mail messages.

- **Notification E-Mail**: This is the e-mail address to which to send endpoint update notification e-mail messages.

- **E-Mail From Address**: This is the address that will show up as sender in notification messages sent.

- **E-Mail Subject**: This is the text to display in the subject line of notification e-mail messages.

- **E-Mail Body**: This is the text for the body of notification e-mail messages.

- **Contact Name**: This setting is name of the UDDI administrator to notify of endpoint update requests.

- **Contact E-Mail**: This setting is used for the e-mail address of the UDDI administrator for notifications of endpoint update requests.

The following screenshot shows all of the settings mentioned in preceding list:

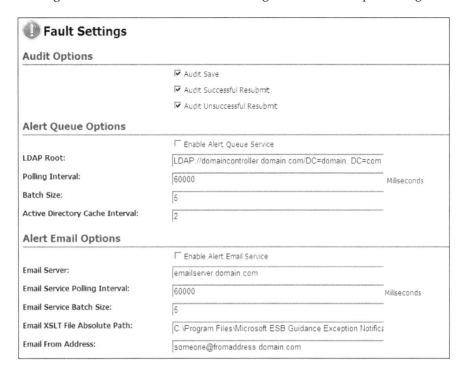

In the ESB Management Portal, we can see in the top menu an entry that takes us to the **Registry** functionality, shown in the following screenshot:

On this view, we can directly register a service into UDDI. To do this, first we have to search the endpoint that we want to publish. These can be endpoints of services that the ESB consumes through **Send ports**, or endpoints of services that the ESB exposes through receive locations.

As an example, we will publish one of the services exposed by the ESB through the `GlobalBank.ESB` sample application that comes with the ESB Toolkit.

First, we will search on the **New Registry Entry** page for the endpoints in the `GlobalBank.ESB` application, as shown in the following screenshot:

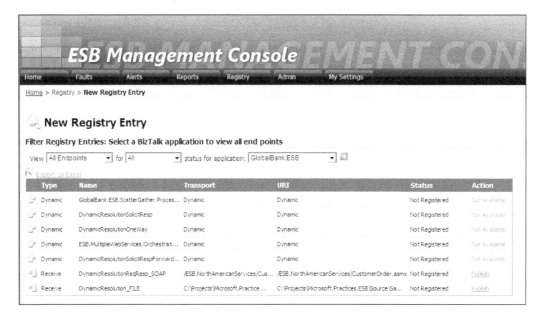

Once we get the results, we will click on the **Publish** link of the `DynamicResolutionReqResp_SOAP` endpoint that actually exposes the `/ESB.NorthAmericanServices/CustomerOrder.asmx` service. We will be presented with a screen where we can fill in further details about the service registry entry, such as the service provider under which we want to publish the service (or we can even create a new service provider that will get registered in UDDI as well).

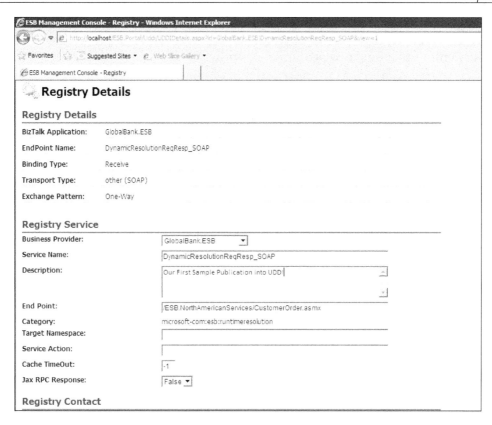

After clicking on the **Publish** button at the bottom of the page, we will be directed back to the **New Registry Entry** screen, where we can filter again and see how our new registry entry is in **Pending** status, as it needs to be approved by an administrator.

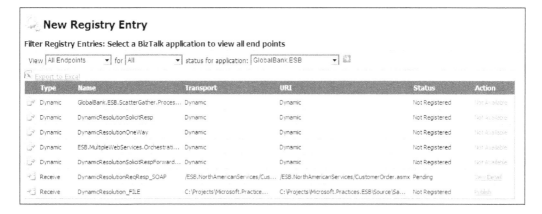

We can access the **Manage Pending Requests** module through the corresponding submenu under the top-level **Registry** menu. There we can see if there are any new registry entries that might be pending for approval.

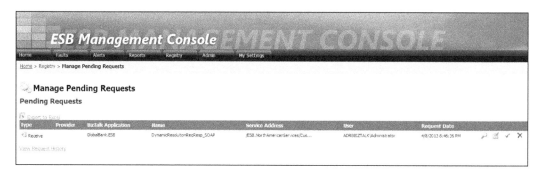

By using the buttons to the left of each item, we can view the details of the request, edit them, and approve or delete the request.

Once we approve the request, we will receive a confirmation message on the portal telling us that it got approved. Then, we can go to the UDDI portal and look for the service provider that we just created, where we will see that our service got registered.

The following screenshot shows how the service provider of the service we just published is shown in the UDDI portal:

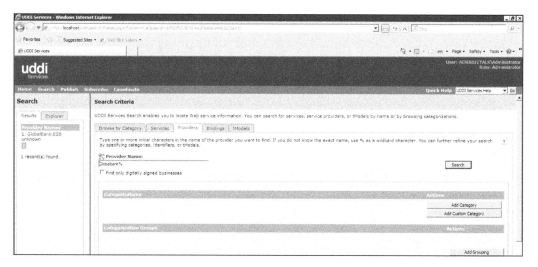

In the following screenshot we can see the actual service published, with its corresponding properties.

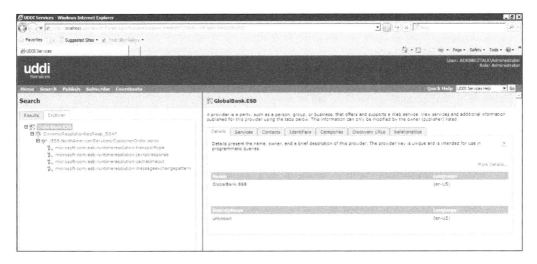

With these simple steps, we can easily build our own services registry in UDDI based on the services our organization already has, so they can be used by the ESB or any other systems to discover services and know how to consume them.

Understanding the Audit Log

Audit Log is a small reporting feature that is meant to provide information about the status of messages that have been resubmitted to the ESB through the resubmission module that we saw in *Chapter 3*, *ESB Exception Handling*. We can access this module through the **Manage Audit Log** menu.

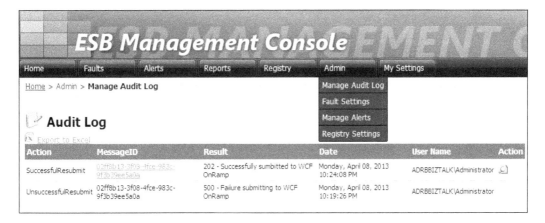

We will be presented with a list of the messages that were resubmitted, if those were resubmitted successfully or not, and even check the actual message that was resubmitted, as the message could have been modified before being resubmitted.

Fault Settings

On the **Fault Settings** page we can specify:

- **Audit Options**: This includes the type of events that we want to audit:
    ◦ **Audit Save**: When a message associated with a fault is saved.
    ◦ **Audit Successful Resubmit**: When a message is successfully resubmitted.
    ◦ **Audit Unsuccessful Resubmit**: When the resubmission of a message fails.

- **Alert Queue Options**: Here we can enable or disable the queuing of the notifications generated when a fault message is published to the portal.

- **Alert Email Options**: Here we can enable and configure the service that will actually send e-mail notifications once fault messages are published to the portal. The three most important settings in this section are:
    ◦ **Email Server**: The e-mail server that will be actually used to send the e-mails.
    ◦ **Email From Address**: The address that will show up as sender in the e-mails sent.
    ◦ **Email XSLT File Absolute Path**: The XSLT transformation sheet that will be used to format the e-mails. The ESB Toolkit provides one, but we could customize it or create our own sheet according to our requirements.

ⓘ Fault Settings

Audit Options

☑ Audit Save

☑ Audit Successful Resubmit

☑ Audit Unsuccessful Resubmit

Alert Queue Options

☐ Enable Alert Queue Service

LDAP Root:	LDAP ://domaincontroller.domain.com/DC=domain. DC=com
Polling Interval:	60000 Milliseconds
Batch Size:	5
Active Directory Cache Interval:	2

Alert Email Options

☐ Enable Alert Email Service

Email Server:	emailserver.domain.com
Email Service Polling Interval:	60000 Milliseconds
Email Service Batch Size:	5
Email XSLT File Absolute Path:	C.\Program Files\Microsoft ESB Guidance Exception Notifica
Email From Address:	someone@fromaddress.domain.com

Summary

In this chapter, we discussed the additional features of the ESB Management Portal.

We learned about the registry settings, which are used for configuring the UDDI and setting up the e-mail notifications. We also learned how to configure fault settings and how to utilize the Audit Log features.

6

ESB Toolkit Version 2.2 for BizTalk 2013

In this chapter, we will discover what's new in ESB Toolkit Version 2.2, and how to install and configure it.

We will also walk through installing and configuring the ESB Management Portal sample that is provided with the toolkit.

What's new

The new features in ESB Toolkit Version 2.2 are:

- BizTalk Server 2013 now includes the ESB Toolkit 2.2. It is no longer a separate application that we need to download and install.

- Installation and configuration is much simpler.

Installing the ESB Toolkit 2.2

The ESB Toolkit is no longer a separate installation. It is now an installation option included with BizTalk 2013, as shown in the following screenshot:

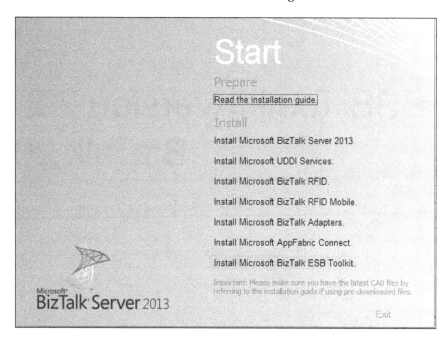

Configuring the ESB Toolkit 2.2

After installing the ESB Toolkit 2.2, we need to configure it. We will use the ESB Configuration Tool. In order to start the tool we must select it from the new Windows **User Interface (UI)**.

The ESB configuration is based upon using Microsoft Windows Server 2012.

Press the Windows key to switch to new Windows **User Interface (UI)** and then type esb as shown in the following screenshot:

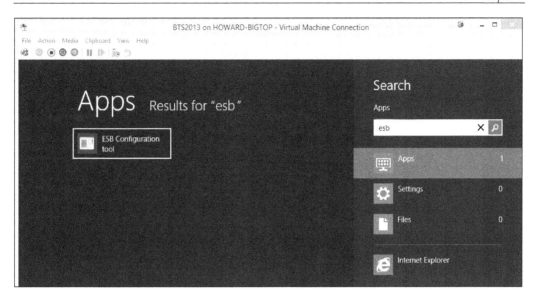

Once we have clicked on **ESB Configuration tool** in the **Apps** menu, the tool
is started on our Desktop as shown in the following screenshot:

As you can see, the configuration is similar to the one in ESB Toolkit 2.1 with the following differences:

- We can do a basic configuration by entering the information in the configuration tab as shown in the preceding screenshot. We then click on the **Apply Configuration** button and our services are deployed and configured.

- We can customize our configuration of the Exception Management and ESB Core Services separately as was done in ESB Toolkit 2.1.

Performing a custom configuration

In order for to perform a custom configuration we must follow certain steps.

Configuring the Exception Management Database

The following are the steps we take to configure the ESB databases and services:

1. We start off by configuring the Exception Management Database as shown in the following screenshot. Check the **Enable Exception Management Database** checkbox.

2. Both the **Database server name** and **Database name** values will be auto-populated.

3. We have the option to change the **BizTalk Admin Group** and **BizTalk App Group** names.

4. Click on the **Apply Configuration** button to apply the changes.

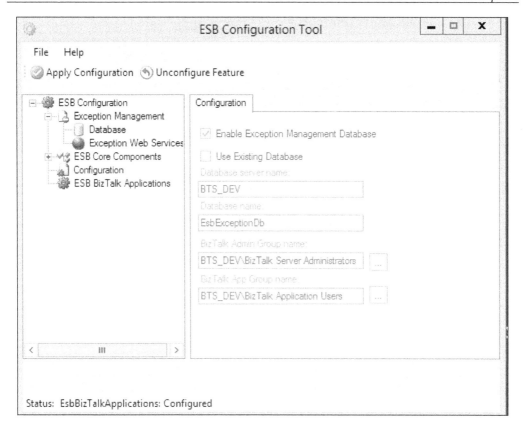

Configuring the Exception Service

Next configure the Exception Service as shown in the following screenshot:

1. Click on the **Enable Exception Services** button.

2. We have the option of selecting values for **User Account**, **BizTalk Isolated Host Group**, and **Website name**.

3. We also have the option of selecting the type of **Handling Service**, either **ASMX** or **WCF**, or both.

4. Click on the **Apply Configuration** button to apply the changes.

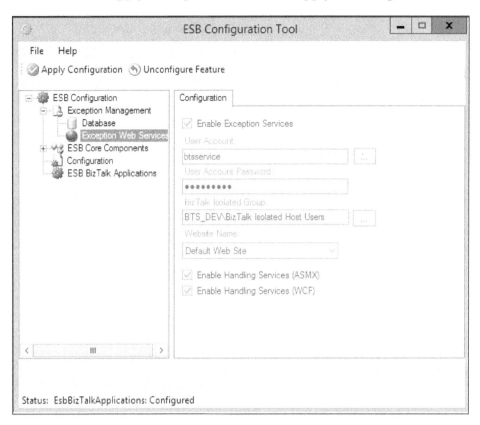

Configuring the Itinerary Database

Then we configure the Itinerary Database as shown in the following screenshot:

1. Click on the **Itinerary** button.

2. We have the option to set the name for **BizTalk Isolated Host Group**, **BizTalk App Group**, and **BizTalk Server Admin Group**.

3. Click on the **Apply Configuration** button to apply the changes.

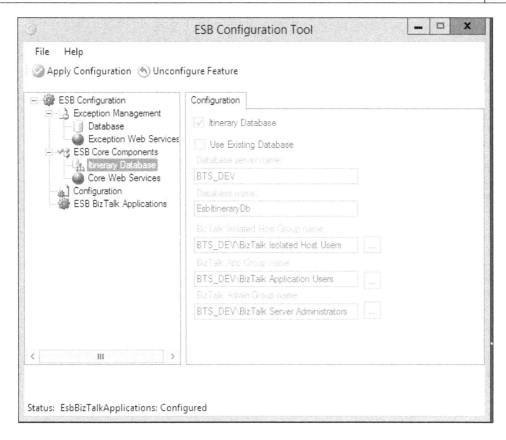

Configuring some Core Web Services

Our Core Web Services are configured as shown in the following screenshot:

1. Click on the **Enable Core Services button**.

2. Next configure **User Account, BizTalk Isolated Host Group, and select the Website name**.

3. We can select one or more of the following services:

   ° **Transformation Services**

   ° **Operation Services**

   ° **Resolution Services**

   ° **Itinerary Services**

4. Then click on the **Apply Configuration** button to apply the changes.

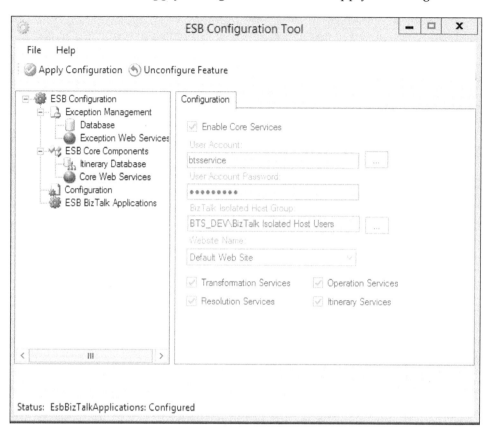

Setting our Configuration Source

1. We have a choice of using the File or SSO configuration source. **Select File Configuration Source** as shown in the following screenshot:

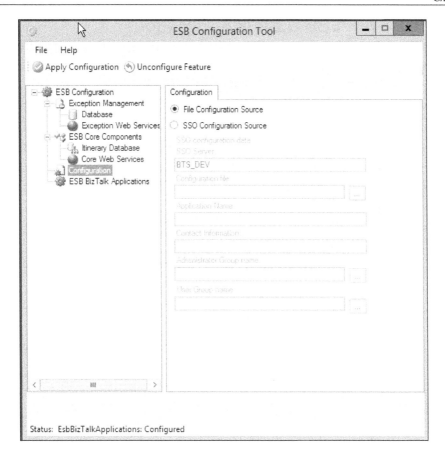

 The File configuration source is commonly used for non-production environments. For secure environments, like production, SSO should be selected.

Confguring our ESB BizTalk Applications

There is a new configuration option in the tool, **ESB BizTalk Applications**. We use this configuration to enable ESB core components and/or JMS/WMQ components in BizTalk Server 2013 as shown in the following screenshot:

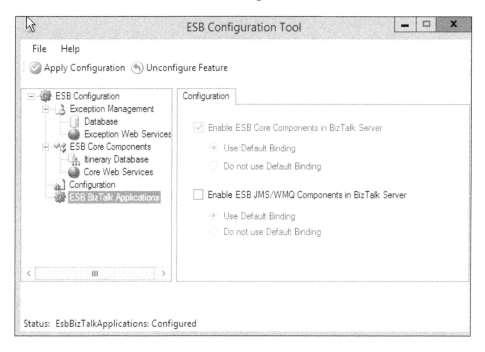

By enabling the Core Components, and clicking on **Apply Configuration**, they are deployed to the BizTalk Server. We also have the choices: **Use Default Binding** or **Do not use Default Binding**.

The ESB Core Components consist of the Microsoft.Practices. ESB BizTalk Server application. All the Core Web Services we previously configured will be deployed and bound. If the Exception Web Services were configured, they would also be deployed and bound.

If we select **Use Default Binding** the standard binding included with the ESB Toolkit is used. Otherwise, if we select **Do not use Default Binding**, the components are installed, but not bound. This allows us to use a custom binding file.

Installing and configuring the Management Portal Sample Solution

We will need to open the Management Portal Sample Solution in Visual Studio 2012.

The Management Portal Sample Solution has the setup projects that were used in Visual Studio 2010. Unfortunately the use of setup projects has been removed in Visual Studio 2012. These projects still exists in the samples provided with the toolkit. We will need to delete them from the solution.

If we try to build the solution, we will get errors

First we will need to install the Enterprise Library 5.0, which is available at `www.microsoft.com/en-my/download/details.aspx?id=15104`.

We will also need to install Microsoft Report Viewer Redistributable 2008 which is downloadable from `www.microsoft.com/en-us/download/details.aspx?id=577`.

> Mike Diiorio has an excellent article on his blog, `mikediiorio.net/2013/04/08/configure-biztalk-esb-toolkit-2-2-management-portal/`, that will provide us with step-by-step instructions to correct these errors and get the ESB Management Portal configured.

Summary

In this chapter, we discovered what's new in the ESB Toolkit 2.2. We also saw that Microsoft simplified how the Toolkit is installed and configured. We found out that the ESB Toolkit 2.2 Management Portal sample needs some tweaking before we could build and deploy it.

Index

Itinerary.Response.SOAP 74-76
Itinerary.Response.WCF 76
Itinerary Selector pipeline component
   used with dynamic resolution, for executing
      itinerary 49
   used with static resolution, for executing
      itinerary 49
itinerary services
   about 13, 18, 22
   registering 48
   tracking 36, 37
   types 22
ItineraryServices.Generic.Response.WCF 77
ItineraryServices.Generic.WCF 77
itinerary services, types
   messaging services 22
   off-ramp extenders 22
   orchestration services 22
Itinerary.SOAP 74-76
itinerary state
   retrieving 43, 44
ITINERARY-STATIC resolver
   about 28
   Name property 28
   Version property 28
itinerary step
   completing 46
itinerary structure
   about 19
   itinerary metadata instance 20
   itinerary model 20
Itinerary.WCF 76
Itinerary web services
   about 73
   Itinerary.Response.SOAP 74-76
   Itinerary.Response.WCF 76
   ItineraryServices.Generic.Response.WCF
      77
   ItineraryServices.Generic.WCF 77
   Itinerary.SOAP 74-76
   Itinerary.WCF 76

L

LDAP resolver 28

M

Management Portal Sample Solution
   configuring 103
   installing 103
mapping service 29
message
   processing 43, 45
   receiving 42, 43
MessageFlowTree method 81
message, processing
   itinerary state, retrieving 43, 44
   itinerary step, completing 46
Message Viewer 69
messaging itinerary service
   about 28, 29
   custom itinerary services, creating on 39-41
messaging runtime
   fault message, originating by 55
messaging services 22
methods, Exception Handling API
   about 59
   AddMessage 59
   CreateFaultMessage method 59
   GetException 60
   GetMessage 60
   GetMessages 60
   SetException 59
Microsoft BizTalk Server 2006 R2 9
Microsoft.Practices.ESB BizTalk application
   23
Microsoft Report Viewer Redistributable
   2008
   installing 103
Moniker 25

N

New Registry Entry page 86
Notification E-Mail option 84
Notification Enabled option 84

O

off-Ramp ESB Extender
   about 24
   BizTalk Application property 24
   Send Port property 24

Thank you for buying
Microsoft BizTalk ESB Toolkit 2.1

About Packt Publishing

Packt, pronounced 'packed', published its first book "Mastering phpMyAdmin for Effective MySQL Management" in April 2004 and subsequently continued to specialize in publishing highly focused books on specific technologies and solutions.

Our books and publications share the experiences of your fellow IT professionals in adapting and customizing today's systems, applications, and frameworks. Our solution based books give you the knowledge and power to customize the software and technologies you're using to get the job done. Packt books are more specific and less general than the IT books you have seen in the past. Our unique business model allows us to bring you more focused information, giving you more of what you need to know, and less of what you don't.

Packt is a modern, yet unique publishing company, which focuses on producing quality, cutting-edge books for communities of developers, administrators, and newbies alike. For more information, please visit our website: www.packtpub.com.

About Packt Enterprise

In 2010, Packt launched two new brands, Packt Enterprise and Packt Open Source, in order to continue its focus on specialization. This book is part of the Packt Enterprise brand, home to books published on enterprise software – software created by major vendors, including (but not limited to) IBM, Microsoft and Oracle, often for use in other corporations. Its titles will offer information relevant to a range of users of this software, including administrators, developers, architects, and end users.

Writing for Packt

We welcome all inquiries from people who are interested in authoring. Book proposals should be sent to author@packtpub.com. If your book idea is still at an early stage and you would like to discuss it first before writing a formal book proposal, contact us; one of our commissioning editors will get in touch with you.

We're not just looking for published authors; if you have strong technical skills but no writing experience, our experienced editors can help you develop a writing career, or simply get some additional reward for your expertise.

SOA Patterns with BizTalk Server 2009

ISBN: 978-1-84719-500-5   Paperback: 400 pages

Implement SOA strategies for BizTalk Server solutions

1. Discusses core principles of SOA and shows them applied to BizTalk solutions

2. The most thorough examination of BizTalk and WCF integration in any available book

3. Leading insight into the new WCF SQL Server Adapter, UDDI Services version 3, and ESB Guidance 2.0

Microsoft BizTalk Server 2010 Patterns

ISBN: 978-1-84968-460-6   Paperback: 396 pages

Create effective, scalable solutions with Microsoft BizTalk Server 2010

1. Provides a unified example from the beginning to end of a real world solution

2. A starter guide expecting little or no previous BizTalk experience, but offering advanced concepts and techniques

3. Provides in-depth background and introduction to the platform and technology

Please check **www.PacktPub.com** for information on our titles

BizTalk Server 2010 Cookbook

ISBN: 978-1-84968-434-7   Paperback: 368 pages

Over 50 recipes for developers and administrators looking to deliver well-built BizTalk solutions and environments

1. Enhance your implementation skills with practically proven patterns

2. Written by a BizTalk expert and MVP, Steef-Jan Wiggers, the book is filled with practical advice

3. Learn best practices for deploying BizTalk 2010 solutions

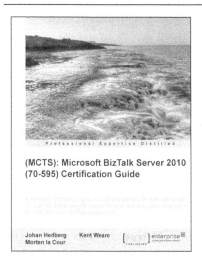

(MCTS): Microsoft BizTalk Server 2010 (70-595) Certification Guide

ISBN: 978-1-84968-492-7   Paperback: 476 pages

A compact certification guide to help you prepare for and pass exam 70-595: TS: Developing Business Process and Integration Solutions by Using Microsoft BizTalk Server 2010

1. This book and e-book will provide all that you need to know in order to pass the (70-595) Developing Business Process and Integration Solutions exam by Using Microsoft BizTalk Server 2010 book

2. Includes a comprehensive set of test questions and answers that will prepare you for the actual exam

3. The layout and content of the book closely matches that of the skills measured by the exam, which makes it easy to focus your learning and maximize your study time in areas where you need improvement

Please check **www.PacktPub.com** for information on our titles

www.ingramcontent.com/pod-product-compliance
Lightning Source LLC
LaVergne TN
LVHW080059070326
832902LV00014B/2325